Inviting God into Your Life

A PRACTICAL GUIDE FOR PRAYER

William M. Watson, S.J.

Paulist Press
New York/Mahwah, N.J.

IMPRIMATUR
+ George V. Murry, S.J.
Bishop of St. Thomas

Cover & book design by Lynn Else

Library of Congress Cataloging-in-Publication Data

Watson, William M.
    Inviting God into your life : a practical guide for prayer / William M. Watson.
      p. cm.
    Includes bibliographical references.
    ISBN 0-8091-4137-X
    1. Prayer—Christianity. I. Title.
    BV210.3 .W395 2003
    248.3′2—dc21

2003004419

Published by Paulist Press
997 Macarthur Boulevard
Mahwah, New Jersey 07430

www.paulistpress.com

Printed and bound in the United States of America

Contents

The Great Mission of Christianity

My twenty years of retreat work and spiritual direction have shown me that most people have little sense that they are called to be part of a great mission. But in reality, the message of our Catholic Christian faith is also a mission for you and me.

The success of the film *Star Wars* in the 1980s was not surprising to me. It employed great new visual technologies that engaged the viewer, but the movie's real success was George Lucas's ability to tell the story of a great mission of a battle of good against evil in a way accessible to millions of people around the world. Luke Skywalker, whose very name suggests something impossible, is the young hero who must battle the dark forces. His mission is to undo the threat to galactic civilization. That threat was unleashed by the actions of his own father, a man coopted by evil forces to use power, not for good, but for selfish means.

Almost twenty years after Lucas's story hit screens worldwide, the film version of Tolkien's, *The Lord of the Rings* made its debut. In many respects, Tolkien's vision of a great mission of good battling evil is much more serious and compelling. Tolkien, a devout Roman Catholic, was caught in the terror of the Second World War when he set out to write his mythic story. Steeped in the truth and mysteries of his faith, he knows that the terror of evil inflicted upon humanity is overcome at the price of the sacrifice of the Son of God. Tolkien could see the price of that victory played out before him in the almost unspeakable violence of war-torn Europe and in the sacrifice of the tens of thousands of lives it took to turn back the Nazi forces. The violence and evil touched Tolkien's native England as well, and many of his friends were killed in that war.

Tolkien's depiction of good battling evil is better than Lucas's, I believe, because Tolkien is more connected to the reality of the battle in both the material world and in the supernatural realm. The book (and the film) provide many of us living in an age dulled by technology and the consequent loss of a sense of the supernatural and the transcendent realm a new access to the heart of the Christian missionary message. What, in essence, is the Christian message and its missionary call?

In mythic, broad outline, it is this: In the beginning, God created the heavens and the earth and *all things seen and unseen.* Included in God's creation are the principalities and powers, the angels, the archangels, and man and woman. Man and woman, the height of God's creation created in God's own loving image, are endowed with free will. They were created in love and destined to share God's life and love forever.

Lucifer, the "light bearer," the greatest angel commissioned to stand next to the Eternal Light, the second person of the Trinity, refuses to cooperate with the divine plan of love for the universe. Convincing many in the heavenly realm to turn from God's plan for creation, Lucifer, along with his followers, is cast out of the presence of God forever. Choosing anti-love for a mission, Lucifer seeks to destroy all of God's creation, especially humankind: man and woman.

Satan, the Prince of Darkness, tempts man and woman to use their free choice to serve not pure Love, but their own selfish desires. Because of their free choice, violence, greed, betrayal, death, and destruction enter paradise. God's plan is upended and Satan's mission to destroy creation looks assured.

But God does not intend to abandon his beloved creation to the power of darkness and eternal death. In God's great love, the Son will be sent to battle the power of Lucifer.... *The Son of God was revealed for this purpose, to destroy the works of the devil* (1 John 3:8b). The perfect love and obedience of the Son become human will once again open the way to paradise and eternal life. The refusal to love God that occasioned the first sin and all that followed can now be forgiven by the Son's selfless sacrifice.

He has rescued us from the power of darkness and transferred us into the kingdom of his beloved Son, in whom we have redemption, the forgiveness of sins. (Col 1:13–14)

But similar to Tolkien's story, God will choose the weak to help realize the great plan to save the universe and humanity. In choosing mortal humans for this greatest of missions, God must help them overcome their fear, convince them that what for them seems impossible is not impossible for God, and finally get them to trust completely in the faithfulness of God's power to work through their human weakness. Overcoming great fear, surrendering to the impossible, and trusting in the power of God; this is the Christian pattern of mission and vocation as laid out in the very beginning of the gospel stories.

Mary, visited by an angel, is deeply troubled by his words. She does not understand how she is to conceive, but she is told not to fear. Her offspring will be called great, the Son of God Most High. Mary cooperates with the plan offered by God through Gabriel.

Joseph, knowing Mary to be pregnant, decides to divorce her quietly. In a dream, he is visited by an angel and told not to fear taking Mary as his wife. He cooperates with a plan that for him seems impossible.

Zechariah, worshiping in the temple at the incense hour, is also visited by an angel. He is deeply disturbed upon seeing him and overcome by fear. He is given a mission to name his son John. Zechariah, knowing Elizabeth is beyond childbearing years, views this as impossible. He does not believe and is struck dumb by the angel.

Mary is praised by her cousin Elizabeth for believing that the promises made to her would be fulfilled. Mary in turn praises God who "...*has scattered the proud in the thoughts of their hearts. He has brought down the powerful from their thrones, and lifted up the lowly...*" (Luke 1:51–52). Zechariah's relatives, at the birth of Elizabeth's child, are shocked when she decides to name him John, for no one in the family has that name. Zechariah's voice, restored to announce to the assembled family that he affirms the naming of his son John, creates in them great alarm. Scripture records that *"fear came over all their neighbors"* (Luke 1:65).

Mary gives birth to a child who is conceived in her womb, not by the urging of the flesh, nor by sin or the power of man, but by the power of God alone. And on the holy night of the child's birth, the shepherds tending their sheep are visited by angels. Terrified by the visitation, they are encouraged not to be afraid, for the promised Messiah has been born.

The Son, when he comes of age, gathers round him a group of disciples who are to share in his mission. They, too, are often fearful and do not understand what God is asking of them. Eventually, as the mission unfolds, many believe in the Son, but those to whom he is sent reject him and his message. Working through the choices and actions of human instruments, Satan murders the Son of God.

Once again, all seems lost. But because of his perfect obedience and trust in the Father, Jesus is raised to life by the power of the Father. His death and resurrection, far from ending the hope for eternal life and love for humankind, become the very vehicle for humanity's redemption in the forgiveness of sins.

And the Eucharist Jesus gives us on the final, fateful night of his mission, more powerful than any ring, good or evil, is the eternal presence of his life poured out in love for us on the cross. It is his full physical presence—body, blood, soul, and divinity—given to us forever till time ceases to exist. He has given us not a magical object, but his very self, so that his mission of love overcoming evil can be accomplished by all who believe in him and join forces with him.

All the main characters in the Christian story as it progresses in the Gospels must overcome their fear, accept an impossible mission that can only be fulfilled by God's power, and trust that the plan will be fulfilled by a faithful God. Even Jesus, the Son of God, must follow this road. But the human players are the least likely players to succeed in the greatest mission ever conceived.

Frodo, too, in Tolkien's *Ring*, is the most vulnerable and least likely of the characters to accept a great mission to undo the evil in the world. He has to overcome his fear, accept an impossible mission, and trust in the faithfulness of God, as communicated to him through many good spirits, including an angelic Marian figure, the Lady of the Forest.

The *Ring* is helpful in getting Christians back in touch with the true, mythic nature of our faith and the reality of good and evil in the world. But the Christian story is even more fantastic than Tolkien's masterpiece because the Christian story is true. The Prince of Peace, the Son of Justice, the Lord of Love has entered human history to undo violence, death, and evil, and he seeks followers to share in his mission. Each of us, as members of the Body of Christ, is given a specific mission to help the Son of God bring about his kingdom of love and justice.

… Go therefore and make disciples of all nations, baptizing them in the name of the Father and of the Son and of the Holy Spirit, and teaching them to obey everything that I have commanded you. And remember, I am with you always, to the end of the age. (Matt 28:19–20)

Whether you are fourteen or eighty-four, you are invited to take part in the Son's great mission. Remember, too, that God chooses the weak and makes them strong in bearing witness to Christ in the world. Each one reading this has fears of entering more deeply in the Christian mystery and mission. This is natural. Each one of us is incapable of conceiving of how the deepest desires in our hearts for love and peace in the world can ever come to pass. Many of us are frightened of committing to a path of love and forgiveness, for it seems the powerful and violent will destroy us. Love and forgiveness seem too weak a response in the face of violence so powerful. But do not fear. Trust, like Mary, that the promise in your heart will be fulfilled.

This little book is dedicated to everyone seeking a mission in life. It is written so that those who want to commit more deeply to the Son's mission of love, justice, peace, and truth can find him more easily in their daily lives.

Besides this, you know what time it is, how it is now the moment for you to wake from sleep. For salvation is nearer to us now than when we became believers; the night is far gone, the day is near. Let us then lay aside the works of darkness and put on the armor of light. (Rom 13:11–12)

The Lord counts on you to help complete his mission against evil in the world and to bring about his kingdom of peace. I greet you, fellow companion, in his name, the Lord of justice and peace, the Lord of life and love, our brother and Savior, Jesus the Christ. May he be your daily bread and enduring peace.

Bill Watson, S.J.
Christmas Day, 2001

PART ONE

Beginnings

Happiness and Peace—two gifts that everyone wants. But I have discovered that these two gifts are rarities in the life of the average Christian. Is this because they are hard to find or impossible human goals? I don't think so. My own work tells me that the rarity of happiness and peace is more a result of a weak spiritual life. And the weakness of the spiritual life is more often than not connected to a person's inability to know how or where to begin a relationship with God that nourishes the heart and mind.

How to begin? Jesus shows us the way when he invites us to live in his love. What Jesus proposes is neither elaborate nor complicated. Simply this: We are to live in his love.

Gathered in this booklet is a sampling of the simplest but most effective pathways to connect with God in daily life. Most of the sections have been influenced by my retreat work with high school and college students, university faculty, and alumni. The rest of the booklet contains spiritual wisdom and advice that I have found holds universal appeal to all age groups seeking growth in the Christian life. All of it is intended as a means to draw you deeper into God's love. This divine love is offered to you every single moment of your life. It is most completely offered in the Eucharist.

We each need to find a path to pray daily in order to live in God's love. Prayer, simply stated, is both the ways you relate to God and allow God to touch your life. Your relationship with God is the one sure way of easing your difficulties. It will point the way to hope and heighten your knowledge of your deepest self. Prayer will lead you to personal freedom and also heal your broken spirit and relationships. Prayer will help you find your course in life and open to you the way to eternal life. Prayer connects you to the heart of God, who is your Daily Bread and enduring peace.

Developing your relationship with God is well worth the daily effort and time it requires. It does require *daily* effort. But investing in your relationship with God (yes, it is an "investment" and the most significant one possible) will have more lasting effects on the shape and course of your life than anything else that you do. Consider how complicated and stressful your life gets when you are cut off from your heart.

In all honesty, what takes the greater effort? Living a stressed life or taking some time each day to let God lift your burdens?

Your Mission

Your life is in reality a mission leading to eternal life. God is the origin of, the reason for, as well as the journey's destination. Where are you on the journey? Perhaps you have just finished making a retreat and want to bring the spirit of prayer and reflection back into your daily life. You may be preparing for entrance into the church through the RCIA program at your parish or school, or you may have recently become Catholic and are looking for ways to make your new faith a regular part of your life. Perhaps you are a high school or college student who wants to learn how to begin a simple relationship with God. Maybe you are experienced in the spiritual life but want to touch base with some of the basic building blocks of Christian spirituality. Then again, you might be someone completely new to any kind of personal prayer.

Whatever your age and wherever you find yourself in your faith journey, consider the next step God is inviting you to take in your mission. Examine the different ways of praying presented here and find one that will take you that next step along the road. How to choose? Just pay close attention to the prayers presented here that hold special appeal when you read them. Use your intuition, draw upon what is helpful, and set aside for a while the things that seem unproductive. But daily exercise your spirit in some way, even if it is only for a few minutes. Jesus entered into human history, lived, taught, suffered, and died to give you the gift of life.

The gift of living in God's love and serving alongside Jesus in his mission awaits your daily response. What wonders you will discover as you go further on your mission—wonders of peace and happiness, meaning and fulfillment. A *simple* prayer life *daily* practiced will transform you in ways beyond your imaginings. You will discover why you were placed on this earth and uncover the ultimate mysteries of life.

1.

Six Practical Tips for All Forms of Prayer

One: Simplicity and Regularity

The kinds of prayer presented here are simple. My advice is to leaf through the book and find that one style of prayer that just feels right for you at this point in your life. The form of prayer you choose should be something you think you can manage once a day. Make a commitment to your daily relationship with God in this way for a month's time.

If you try something too elaborate or time consuming, chances are you will not be able to maintain the commitment. If you settle on a simple pattern but don't resolve at the outset to do it regularly, odds are against sustained success. Again, keep it simple and resolve to do it faithfully. Listen to this one more time because it is very important: *Keep it simple and be faithful to your daily ritual.*

Two: Keep Your Time Constant

Some days you will feel God's presence and be given the gift of joy and consolation. Prayer will be easy on these days, and you may want to extend your prayer time. Other days you will be neutral—feeling no particular joy or consolation but not feeling impatient or frustrated either. Praying on these days will seem less rewarding and you will be tempted to shorten your time or to not pray at all. On some days you might be downright discouraged and desolate. God may seem like a vague or even a false memory. On these days, the last thing you may want to do is to spend time "with God" in prayer.

There is a very important rule in the spiritual life. It is this: Do not adjust your prayer time to fit your moods or your emotional state. Praying longer on days when you can "feel" God present and less or not at all on days that are difficult is the quickest way to end your prayer life. If you resolved to spend five minutes daily in some type of prayer, keep to that schedule even though you might feel: (a) you could go on for an hour; or (b) every minute feels an hour long! Learning to be faithful to prayer in good times and in bad is essential.

As your prayer life becomes more regular, even daily, you will come to realize what most great spiritual masters and saints knew: that the greatest spiritual growth often happens during the dry times that seemed barren and empty of grace or insights of any kind. In fact, the times that are the most difficult to pray are usually the times we need to take the extra effort to open ourselves to God. Never forget—God is there whether or not we feel his presence. St. Ignatius urged those making his Spiritual Exercises to lengthen prayer for a minute or so on those days when impatience, desolation, or darkness of spirit have us in their grip. In short, stick to your scheduled time and don't decrease or increase your daily routine unless you first discuss it with a spiritual advisor or confessor.

Three: Trust That God Will Help You

Jesus' life is clear proof that God wants to be in an intimate, trusting, and real relationship with you. Jesus died for you to make a relationship possible. You have been called by name, and God holds you in his hand. You have been carved on the palm of God's hand, as the psalmist says. Even if a mother could forget the child of her womb, God, the psalmist continues, could never forget you. Jesus tells us that he has come so that we can have life and have it to the fullest extent possible. Jesus wants our happiness and peace.

Throughout the New Testament, the evangelists recount Jesus trying to encourage his listeners to develop an intimate and trusting relationship with God. Consider the number of stories in the Gospels about the Father's loving mercy. Remember, Jesus says that blessings will come to those who are patient and faithful to God's word. Remember how much Jesus wants to give us the fullness of life so that we discover our true selves and find in him the hope and peace we desire with all our hearts.

Jesus promises that if we seek first God's kingdom, then we will be given everything else we need. He also promises that the weary will find rest for their souls if they live his way of love and forgiveness. Possibly for the first time in your life, take Jesus seriously in his desire to help you have a real relationship with him. Ask for his help each time you pray and throughout your day whenever you think of it. If you do this, your prayer life will grow and your intimacy with God increase.

Don't ever think that you are bothering God in asking for help. Don't put off asking for help because you think God is too busy with other important things. God has given you his Son, Jesus Christ, as a promise of his fidelity to you. Likewise, the gifts of the Spirit and the sacraments have been given to us through the church so that you can have direct contact with the heart of God. All that is needed now is a simple response on your part. Ask God to help you develop a real relationship with him. I have never, absolutely never, had an experience of asking God for help and being let down. Based on my own personal experience with God and all that I have witnessed as a priest and a spiritual director, I know more surely than anything else in the world that God will give you the help you need if you but ask for it.

Four: Find a Place for Prayer

It is possible to pray anywhere, but your times of prayer can be more fruitful if you find a regular place to pray. Prayer is an intimate way of relating with God. Our most important relationships and their most intimate moments are sacred times, and ritual and routine help us focus our hearts. God does not need rituals, but we do. The ritual and routine of a place for your times of prayer can help you be more attentive to your heart and the quiet voice of God speaking inside of you.

You are blessed if you are close to a quiet church or chapel where you can easily stop in for five or ten minutes for your daily prayer. It is a gift and a grace to be in the presence of the Lord in the Blessed Sacrament. The Constitutions of the Society of Jesus recommend that Jesuits frequently visit the Lord in the Blessed Sacrament in the course of each day.

If a church or chapel is not immediately accessible, find a place that is relatively quiet where TVs, phones, e-mails, and other people will not distract you. Use the same place for prayer as often as possible, and associate that place with your prayer life. Keep there your prayer book, your Bible, a crucifix, a candle, a rosary, a picture of Christ, or other physical reminders of God and your relationship with him. I even have my baptismal certificate close by to remind me of the day I came into the Body of Christ.

I am not suggesting that you remodel your house or apartment or that you need to purchase beautiful or expensive religious objects to create a sacred place of prayer. Your prayer is not "improved" by any accessories you can purchase. But your capacity to listen to your heart and your attentiveness to the quiet voice of the Spirit can be greatly improved if you have a special place for prayer.

So find yourself a prayer corner or a chair that you use only for prayer. Keep it simple but, as much as possible, keep the same place for prayer. If you travel a lot, find places that you associate with your prayer life (a favorite church or chapel, arranging a corner of your hotel room, taking time to stop your car for five or ten minutes, etc.). This will help you bring your prayer life on the road wherever you go.

Five: Distractions in Prayer May Bother You But God Is Never Distracted

You can jumpstart your prayer life and save years of worry by making a point of letting your distracted heart and mind become a pathway to God instead of a roadblock. Just

because we set aside time for God in prayer does not guar-
antee that our hearts and minds will be cleared of all
thoughts and concerns and totally focused on God. Many
people who try to pray regularly get frustrated because they
cannot focus on God. Some may feel they are wasting prayer
time or doing something wrong. Our own sinful actions can
greatly hinder our felt sense of God's presence. I will speak
about this later in the section on discernment. However, we
should be mindful that on this side of the grave, to some
degree, the "cares and worries of the world" and our sinful
and weak human nature prevent the perfect union with God
that our hearts desire.

When you find yourself distracted in prayer (*when* not
if), realize in your heart that God is fully present to you in
your distracted state. Turn your thoughts to him and speak
with him about what is distracting you or occupying your
thoughts. God is Love. Therefore God cannot help being
intensely interested in your life, no matter how preoccupied
you are. God does not hold back his concern and care until you
can give him your complete attention. Because he loves you
absolutely, the Lord is completely and lovingly absorbed by
every single detail of your distracted life. Speak to God about
whatever is in your heart or on your mind, even if you find
your thoughts and distractions offensive. Temptations of
whatever kind, even feelings of anger or lust—everything
should be turned over to the Lord in our conversations with
him in prayer. Nothing in your world can ever keep God
from being completely focused on you. Try, then, to let your
own concerns and distractions become pathways to God and
not walls separating you from him.

Six: Speak Directly to God in Prayer Using a Name That Affects You Personally

Your prayer life will deepen significantly if you take the time to discover the name of God that connects directly to your heart. Speak to God in your prayer often using this name. Take some time to consider the name for God the Father, God the Son, or God the Spirit that you have used in prayer or that you have heard others use, the one that is most intimate or meaningful to you. The name that speaks directly to your heart is one you should use when you pray.

The following names for God may help you get in touch with the one that best opens your heart in prayer: Merciful Father, Loving Father, Almighty Father, Our Father, Father God, Loving Creator, Creator God, God of Love, My God, Holy God, Father of the Poor, God of all Mercy, God of All Compassion, Father of Jesus, Lord Jesus Christ, Lord Jesus, Christ my brother, Christ my king, Christ Jesus, Dear Jesus, Adorable Jesus, Adorable Christ, Good Jesus, Jesus, Merciful Savior, Jesus My Savior, Son of God, Dearest Lord, My Lord, My Lord and My God, Sacred Heart of Jesus, Lamb of God, Good Shepherd, Crucified Savior, Holy Spirit, Spirit of Jesus, Spirit of the Lord, Loving Spirit, Holy Spirit of God, Love of God, Divine Spirit, Creator Spirit.

No matter what type of prayer you do, always speak directly to God using the name for God that is most meaningful for you. God knows *your* name and wants you to speak directly to him with the name that connects immediately with both your heart and mind.

2.

The Examen:
A Day's-End Prayer

The Constitutions of the Jesuit Order written by St. Ignatius require that a Jesuit spend fifteen minutes twice a day in a form of prayer called the Examination of Conscience. The prayer was so important to Ignatius that he once said that even if a Jesuit missed all other spiritual disciplines in his day, he should not miss the *Examen*. One Jesuit spiritual writer calls this traditional Ignatian prayer the examination of consciousness.

The word *consciousness* conveys to contemporary Christians this prayer's deeper meaning. What Ignatius wants a Jesuit to cultivate twice daily is consciousness of the presence of God in his life as well as how he has responded to God that day. This is why it is so important to do regularly, especially if one misses all other spiritual disciplines. Forgetting about God is one of the most common spiritual ailments in the Christian life.

If you take the time to open your heart and mind to God even once a day with the intention of examining how God's grace has been present and how you have (or have not) responded to that grace, your spiritual life and response to God will grow significantly. And if you missed all your other spiritual disciplines that day, you will probably discover the reason why.

When you take time to ask God to help you to listen to the deepest part of your heart, you can *examine and become conscious* of what causes true joy and peace. You will also discover those things that are robbing you of freedom and hope. Surprisingly, most people I have encountered in my years as a priest and spiritual director lack this basic knowledge of the heart. Many also lack an awareness of God's presence in their lives.

The goal of the Christian life is to grow in union with God. Becoming conscious of what moves you toward or away from God is absolutely critical if you are to grow spiritually. Praying this way, Ignatius could discern the voice of God within his own heart and experience constant, daily growth in familiarity with God's will and God's presence in his life. You will too.

The Examen helps us cultivate an awareness of both the grace and the sin in our lives. Now you may feel positive about the *blessing* side of the equation, but most of us are fearful of our *sinfulness* and of seeking forgiveness and healing when we fall short of love. But listen very carefully: Contrary to making you feel discouraged, the awareness of your failings *in light of God's love for you* will significantly increase your peace, hope, and trust. You will learn that your very identity, security, and peace are based not on your ability to be perfect, but on God's perfect mercy and love for you *in your weakness*.

A growth in the knowledge of your weak and sinful nature won't make you grow slack in your spiritual quest nor will it discourage you. Your growing awareness and gratitude of Jesus who loved you "while you were still a sinner" will work to increase your desire both to serve and to love.

Remember that God is the one who prays *in you*. As you begin your Examen, call upon God's grace to touch your memory and conscience. God will give you sensitivity to your own spirit—its longings, its powers, and its source in the Holy Spirit. If you are faithful to the Examen prayer you will gradually develop an awareness of God's many blessings in your life and also how particular temptations and patterns of sin cut you off from your true self.

The pattern detailed below will help you understand the Examen prayer and its basic outline. Read the ritual over enough times to learn the *substance* of each section. To help you with the third movement, you might want to refresh your memory with the examination of conscience from part 1, section 4 of this book.

Become familiar with the parts of the Examen so that when you do it at midday or at the end of the day, you won't need to read from a sheet. (Even though I call it a day's-end prayer, it might fit your schedule better at midday. Or do it twice a day as recommended by St. Ignatius in the Jesuit Constitutions).

If you decide to do the Examen daily or twice daily, determine ahead of time how long you want to spend on it (five, ten, or fifteen minutes). Whenever you do it or for however long, approach this prayer as a *natural conversation* with the Lord, not a mechanical, step-by-step process. If you find yourself doing the steps out of order, don't worry. It is a conversation with God and we don't always have perfect order in our conversations.

Finally, the word *examen* suggests an intellectual activity that *I* initiate. You will notice in looking at the outline below that the Examen prayer asks you to *remember* various aspects of your day—its blessings, etc. So don't spend time trying to *think* too much as you move through the prayer. Trust instead that God will work to touch your memory and surface in your heart what is most important. Let God do the work.

First Movement:
Be Mindful That You Are in God's Presence

No matter how you experience your life at this particular moment, recall that you are a child of God. God's creation is vast but he knows and loves you *personally* by name. Ask God to grace you with an open heart and attentive spirit. *Pause briefly as you ask God for this grace.*

Second Movement:
Give Thanks to God for the Gifts
of Life and of the Day

Spend a moment looking at gifts received. Be very concrete and don't forget the simple gifts of life. Recall the gifts of food, a warm shower, the beauty of a storm or a sunny day, the smile of a stranger, an act of kindness done for you, a letter received from a friend, the gift of the Eucharist at Mass or the forgiveness offered in the sacrament of reconciliation. *Pause briefly and be thankful for what first comes to mind.*

Now spend a moment pondering the fundamental gifts that made it possible for you to move through the day. Recall your particular strengths in times of difficulty, your ability to hope in times of weakness, your sense of humor and your life of faith, your intelligence and health, your family and friends. God has given you these basic gifts to draw you into the fullness of life. *Pause and thank God for the one fundamental gift that first comes to mind.*

Third Movement:
Review Your Day for Personal Failings or Loss of Hope

Ask the Holy Spirit for the grace of seeing your life honestly and compassionately as God sees it. Invoke the Holy Spirit for this grace, speaking out loud if that helps you in your prayer.

Now briefly review the day listening to your heart. What were your hesitations and failings? Did you lose your temper or speak badly about a friend or acquaintance? Can you feel where you acted or failed to act as Christ would have acted in a similar situation? Have you lost hope in a part of your life? Remember that Jesus sits beside you and supports you while you ponder your day in this way. *Pause briefly and consider the first thing along the lines of what has just been described that comes to mind.*

Fourth Movement:
Ask for God's Healing, Mercy, and Forgiveness

Having reviewed your day with Jesus by your side, be aware that Jesus looks upon you with compassion. Tell God you need him. In your heart, see Jesus on the cross and tell him the specific things you want him to forgive. *Again, be concrete when you speak to Jesus.* Jesus wants to free you of the burdens of the day. If you realize you need to go to confession for something, resolve to go that week. You give Christ a gift by allowing him to forgive you because the reason he lived, died, and was raised by the Father was to bring you forgiveness and peace. You are taking advantage of what Christ Jesus wants to do for you, and this brings him joy. Realize that Christ is joyful when you trust him enough to forgive you. He knows that you will be happier and more at peace.

Fifth Movement:
Close with the Lord's Prayer

End your Examen by praying the Lord's Prayer. Believe that the Father looks upon you with love as you pray for the coming of the kingdom in your own life and in the world. *Listen closely to the meaning of the words as you pray.*

3.

The Holy Eucharist: God's Agape Feast

Apart from the hope of eternal life, the greatest gift God offers us is the Eucharist. If eternal life is intimate communion with God forever, the Eucharist makes it possible for us to have real communion with Christ Jesus on earth.

The Eucharist is Jesus' fulfillment of the promise he made before his ascension; the promise that he would remain with us till the end of time. He is not only present to us by the gift of the Holy Spirit sent by the Father. Jesus is truly present to us—physically present to us—in this total gift of himself.

The Second Vatican Council says that the celebration of the Eucharist makes present the victory and triumph of Jesus' death. Therefore, the Mass is the pinnacle of the church's activity and the source of all her power. The Lord Jesus is present in four major ways in the Eucharist: in the priest as his representative, in the Scriptures and the Gospel proclaimed, and in the people who gather in God's name. But the Lord Jesus is present physically in the eucharistic elements of bread and wine. His entire glorified being is present in the bread and wine, which have *become* his body and blood. It is not a symbolic presence but a *real* presence.

When we come to Mass, we come to worship God and what God has accomplished in Christ Jesus. We come to worship Christ who is present in our midst. We come to be renewed by the reception of his body and blood so that he will live in us and we will become his ambassadors of love to the world. We come to Mass as individuals and as God's people so that we can be physically present to God in Christ and Christ to us. We need this great gift to better live the mission he has given us to work for his kingdom of justice, love, and peace and to work against all forms of evil and darkness in our lives and in our world.

Have you ever considered the grace and strength you receive from your closest family members and friends when they take time to be with you? Have you considered that they want to be with you, physically present to you, because they love you? Let your understanding of these special moments shared with your loved ones translate into a deeper understanding of the Lord's physical presence to you in the Eucharist. He wants to be with you, physically present to you, because he loves you. And he knows that you need this physical contact with him for the strength to live your life in love. This gift of physical presence is also the Father's blessing to Jesus to allow him to remain *in touch* with those who carry on his mission in the world. Consider how much joy you give to Christ by allowing him to come to you, strengthen you, and renew in you the commitment to live in his love. He is your daily bread and enduring peace.

Our personal connection to Christ is only one aspect of his physical presence in the Eucharist. In and through the eucharistic Christ, we are also physically present to all the saints and the faithful who have gone before us as well as all the members of the body of Christ in the church throughout the world. We are all members of Christ's body connected in *Holy Communion* by the loving presence of Christ Jesus in the Eucharist. And while Holy Communion, through the eucharistic Christ, unites all the faithful in heaven and earth, the Mass itself makes us present to Jesus' supreme act of sacrificial love on Calvary. The holy sacrifice of the Mass continually offered throughout the world makes present, in time and space, *the* act of love that has conquered death, sin, and darkness. The intentions we offer in the Mass for all those situations and people in the world are taken to the heart of God through the real presence of Christ Jesus. By a miracle of grace, history collapses. God allows all the faithful in heaven and on earth and all those we bring to the Mass through our prayer and intentions to be present to Jesus' total gift of self-sacrificing love for the salvation of our soul and for that of the world.

Our growth in holiness and love comes from something much more than a mechanical reception of this sacrament. How could we casually approach the Eucharist that is so personal and intimate? It is the supreme gift of God's love for us. Not understanding what we are doing when we attend and receive the Eucharist robs us of the power and grace it offers. Understanding the incredible presence the Lord makes available to us in the Mass transforms how we prepare ourselves to receive its gifts and graces. We need to prepare ourselves so that our reception is worthy and capable of bearing fruit on our great mission in life.

I suggest a simple routine to prepare for Mass that takes five or ten minutes, or spend fifteen seconds on each of the following seven prayer meditations. You may try this short prayer exercise at home or come early before Mass and do it in the church.

Keep in your heart a word or a short phrase that is the fruit of each of these seven short reflections. Before Mass begins, consciously offer these concerns to Jesus and let the intention of your Mass be for one or more of these concerns. Remember that each Mass makes present to the whole congregation the sacrifice of Jesus on the cross. That is why we call it the holy sacrifice of the Mass. You are uniting your prayer with Jesus, whose sacrifice on the cross is truly present. The Father receives not only Jesus' sacrifice, but also your prayers and intentions (and all the other prayers of the faithful present with you and throughout the world) that are made perfect by the sacrifice of God's Son.

Seven Short Reflections to Prepare for the Eucharist

God's Accepting Love

I stop and listen to my heart to discover what I am bringing to Mass. I try to understand what are the most important issues shaping my life. I realize that God accepts me as I am. God lovingly accepts my life and all that I experience. I bring my life as I find it at this time to Christ in the Eucharist.

God's Creative Love

I stop and try to remember that for which I am grateful: What gifts and blessings have been a part of my day, my week, and my life? What has God given me so that I can give praise and thanks? I bring my thanks to the Lord in the Eucharist.

God's Suffering Love

I stop and listen to where I am suffering or in need. I look at the world and hear the cry of so many of God's children suffering from war, violence, and poverty. I look around me in the church and know that many of these people are suffering in ways not visible to me. I bring the sufferings of the world to the Lord in the Eucharist.

God's Forgiving Love

I stop and see how I have turned from God's love. I try to understand how I have said *no* to the invitation to love and forgive, or how I have failed to live the Gospel in my life. I bring my need for forgiveness to Christ in the Eucharist. If needed, I go to the sacrament of reconciliation to prepare my heart to receive the Eucharist in a worthy manner. I bring my need for forgiveness to Jesus in the Eucharist.

God's Sustaining Love

I make an effort, daily, to bring my life to the Lord in a relationship that is real and meaningful. I realize that my brothers and sisters count on me to stay faithful to this relationship daily. I take some time each day to pray, to give thanks, to open my life and my heart to God. I bring this living relationship with God to the Eucharist.

God's Fulfilling Love

I realize that to follow Jesus means to open my life to God's will as Jesus opened himself to follow the will of the Father. In doing so, I know that I never need be afraid that the

Lord will lead me somewhere that will be contrary to the happiness and fulfillment that my heart desires. I ask to follow the Lord's will in all the circumstances of my life: my relationships, my social life, and my career. I bring to the Eucharist my life and future. I ask God to open me to the vocation that will set me free or to deepen in me the vocation I am living. I bring my Christian vocation—my mission—and the hopes for its fulfillment to the Eucharist.

God's Sacrificial Love

I realize that every time I come to Mass, I stand at the foot of Jesus' cross. The gift of his life poured out for me is made present in each and every Eucharist. In the consecrated bread and wine, Jesus is truly present, not symbolically, but in fact. Jesus is present in his divinity and humanity, and in all his glory before the Father and the heavenly kingdom. This sacrifice is truly the Agape feast of God's love. I bring to the Eucharist my awareness of this gift, and I ask God in Christ Jesus to help me understand more fully how so great a gift is given daily out of love for me. I bring my awareness of standing before Christ on the cross to the Eucharist.

How Often Should You Go to Mass?

Sunday Mass

Make sure to go to Sunday Mass and to go to Mass on holy days of obligation. Many Catholics are not in the habit of regular Sunday Mass attendance. Surveys suggest that less than 50 percent of Catholic Americans go to Mass weekly.

Other surveys suggest the number is closer to only one-third of baptized Catholics. Percentages are similar for college students. The greatest and most precious gift in the entire world is passed over by millions of Catholics.

Daily Mass

Try this spiritual experiment: Spend one month going to Mass one day a week apart from Sunday. Many find this a powerful way to deepen a relationship with Christ. Mass during the week can provide a more reflective atmosphere and enable you to slow down and hear the Lord speaking to you. Prepare in the same way you would for the Sunday Mass, using the prayer exercises above.

4.

The Structure of Temptation and the Joy of Reconciliation: The Two Missions

Many people I work with in spiritual direction have a hard time understanding sin and how it works in their lives. Many also lack an understanding of the two great spiritual forces outside of themselves, each seeking to engage us in a different mission. St. Ignatius, in his *Spiritual Exercises,* calls these two missions *the two standards*. Christ's standard is one of poverty, humility, and bearing the ridicule of the world in order to bring about the Father's kingdom. Satan's standard celebrates the riches of the world, and the honors and pride that makes man, not God, the center of the human project.

Most people know they do things that are wrong, but they lack the understanding of why they do the things they do or how the temptation to act wrongly fits into these two missions or standards described above. Let me present a short reflection on how human sinfulness entered the world (and still enters it through our choices and actions). It will help you be present to your experience with an amazing new awareness of how grace and sin work in your life and how the spirit of God and the spirit of darkness operate.

First, God has a plan and a mission for you. God's loving plan for us as individuals and as his people is not random or governed by chance. It is deliberate and one might even say, strategic. Creation and salvation history have nothing to do with chaos theory. God wants your heart, and he uses love to get your attention. He wants you actively engaged in the mission of the Son in the world. God is purposeful and deliberate in his concern for you. He knows your strengths and the love in your heart and how to move you to choose the option of life. He never wastes an opportunity to confront you with love, peace, and mercy to help you understand your life and the mission of love you are destined to share with Jesus.

It is also important to understand that the Tempter's plan is also deliberate, purposeful, and strategic. He also wants you to share in a mission. Understanding how temptation works and how we fall under its spell is an important step any person's faith life. The Tempter has a plan to separate you from God. He knows your weaknesses and how to trap you and he, likewise, never wastes an opportunity.

If you think of the Tempter as deliberately "playing you" to lead you away from joy, peace, and love, you will have an accurate picture of his intent and purposes. Also, by paying attention to the strategic nature of temptation and the mission you are being seduced to share, you will not dead-end in guilt when examining your life. Instead, you will tend to focus more on how you have fallen prey to the one who seeks your destruction and misery. This knowledge will help you always turn in hope to God, who can rescue you from the "snares of the fowler."

The Tempter is effective largely because he poses options to our confused consciences that "seem" to open the way to life, excitement, and new possibilities for growth. He presents a mission that seems positive. However, as choices and options that promise pleasure, they never, absolutely never, end up pleasurable, never lead us to growth and new life. The initial promise of excitement ends in a deadened spirit. St. Ignatius reminds us in his rules for discerning the different spirits, that the angel of darkness often masquerades as an angel of light to cover his tracks. Here, in the true, mythic verse of Scripture, is how it all began.

In the book of Genesis, God walks in the garden in the cool of the evening expressing in poetic images the complete union man and woman experienced with God. There were no barriers of any kind. They loved and obeyed God. Righteousness and truth governed all relationships in paradise. Adam and Eve walked side by side in loving harmony, for they knew and followed *only* the voice of God. This is the way God intended woman and man to relate to him, to each other and to all of creation. Detailed below is the strategy utilized by the Tempter to turn Adam and Eve from God. Pay close attention to how he works.

First Level—Listening Anew and the Loss of Obedience

Adam and Eve walked in harmony and union with God in paradise. But a whole new reality begins when the serpent, the "other" opposed to God's mission, enters the story. Lucifer, the great angel who opposed God, is cast from heaven along with those spirits who joined with him. Hating God and God's plans, he is determined not only to destroy God's creation but also God's creatures, man and woman, made in God's image. The serpent must insert himself between God and Adam and Eve to tempt them to follow him as he did with the other spirits who stopped listening to God's voice and chose to side with the mission of anti-love. This is the origin of the theological concept of the anti-Christ, the one(s) opposed to God's plan and mission for humankind and the universe.

But for temptation to gain a foothold in paradise, the serpent must first establish a relationship with Adam and Eve, and he does this by "speaking" to them. Eve and Adam open themselves to temptation by "listening" to the serpent. By their very listening to the Tempter, they place his voice and suggestions on equal footing with the voice and commands of God.

We think of Adam and Eve as adults, but our understanding of adulthood has been corrupted by the history of so much sin in the world. Adam and Eve were innocent, like children who are innocent. Evil always seeks to corrupt the innocent by clever and subtle invitations. The corruption begins by first getting the innocent to "listen" to new ideas that ever so subtly violate the order of God's creation, God's plan, and God's mission.

Listening indicates their openness to a relationship with the Tempter and displaces God's voice as the only "voice of the heart." The Latin word for *obey* means to *listen deeply*. This is precisely what Adam and Eve have now failed to do. Inviting into their hearts and minds a new voice divides their hearts and minds. In essence, their inviting in another voice is a failure to be obedient. The first level of sin is a violation of the vow of obedience, for Adam and Eve were to listen only to the voice of God.

Let's think of how this first level of temptation and sin affects children at the "age of reason." Consider good and loving parents whose obedient child is being tempted for the first time. The temptation comes from someone (an adult, another child, the Tempter) as a new and different voice with a new and different offer, perhaps inviting the child to consider a different way of behaving from what they have been taught by their "good" parents. There is always a first time when as young children in possession of reason and will, we first *hear,* and then *listen* to *another voice*—one that is very different from the "good" we know and possess in our hearts.

Second Level—Seeing Anew and the Loss of Chastity

After listening to the voice of the Tempter, Adam and Eve are invited to look with different eyes on their Paradise. The Tempter proposes they "see" the fruit of the Tree of Good and Evil as *good* for eating. Delaying at first to respond, the Tempter appeals to human pride, instructing them that they will be *like gods* if they eat this fruit. Pride turns us from trusting God. Pride is *self*-reliance. Infected with pride, perhaps the man and woman now think the reason God has forbidden them the fruit is so they will remain below him. How could something that *looks* good bring death? As the Tempter urges them to deepen their "looking" at the forbidden tree he utters; "Surely you won't die!" God and his mission for humanity is being challenged not just in the heavens, but in the very physical order of creation and in the hearts of man and woman.

This strategy works. They see the fruit as beautiful and good for eating. The Tempter rejoices. A *desire* has been created where one *never existed* previously. Something completely unnecessary for human happiness, peace, and fulfillment suddenly becomes a "need." The hearts of Adam and Eve turn closer to the new voice as the source of their peace and happiness. But in fact, turning closer to the voice of the Tempter is also a turning toward themselves as the source of happiness—a happiness apart from God and a mission apart from God. In this *seeing anew* and the new desires and needs it creates, lust, the spirit of *unchastity*, enters human history.

Think of children taunting a playmate to try something forbidden, saying, "It is not going to kill you" or, "It is fun!" "And besides, you're not going to be a mamma's girl and do everything you are told, are you?" Or think of when you wanted to experiment or to see *for yourself* whether you had been missing fun things. Don't you remember wondering in your heart whether *it* (whatever it was) was really as bad as you had been told?

If the one tempted succumbs to the new desire or lust that has been created, experimentation to test *it*, and the pleasure *it* promises, must proceed. When any new lust is created, the allure and desire to experiment is overwhelming. At this point in the temptation, Adam and Eve no longer see God's plan as the only possible mission in life. They have heard new voices. Perhaps they now think obedience is limiting and constraining. A new potential within themselves has been awakened and perhaps they are now thinking they should trust this strange and exciting instinct. Maybe the fruit could be very good. They are experiencing that the *freedom to choose* for oneself, apart from God, also brings with it a new sense of personal power. This new personal power is the experience the Tempter promised of being *like god*. It is a potent temptation. Opened before them is a world of possibilities that match the many new urgings so recently awakened. From the spirit of disobedience to that of spiritual unchastity, only one step remains to complete the cycle.

Third Level—Acting Anew and Lust and the Loss of Poverty

Temptation's finale moves the person from the realm of interior disobedience and lustful thoughts to the world of action. Mere possibilities turn into concrete choices. If the one tempted believes that a new, better mission might bring happiness, she must experiment to test the truthfulness of what the new voice has proposed. Adam and Eve thus complete the cycle of the first sin by experimenting and taking what does not belong to them. Taking what does not belong to us and what we do not need is a violation of poverty. For we are to find our riches, our meaning, and our mission in "every word that comes from the mouth of God."

The effects of their action are immediate and catastrophic. They see each other now through their own godlike vision—a vision where each of them, and not God, is at the center of their universes. No longer united heart and mind with God, they see each other's beauty not as God sees it, but as something to be used for personal gain or satisfaction. They hide their nakedness from each other. Not because God has made sex unclean, but because they are fearful their partner will see and know how the loss of innocence has corrupted the designs of the human heart. In their *new knowledge* from the fruit of Good and Evil, the human person, made *in dignity, in the image and likeness of God,* has become an *object*—a means to an end for personal satisfaction.

No longer loving each other perfectly in their God-given dignity, they have to hide. Disobedience, lust, and taking what does not belong to oneself have tainted their relationship (mission) with each other, with God, and from this point forward, every relationship in human history will be scarred to greater or lesser degrees. Man and woman no longer live fully for God but now for themselves. This indeed is a very new mission for humanity: to serve the desires of human pride and not God. The human heart is forever divided. Greed, jealousy, anger, avarice, pride, and all other vices enter history and wreak havoc. And by severing their perfect union with God, paradise is forever lost.

The Legacy of Sin—Excitement Followed by Loss

What Genesis has detailed in the threefold sin of Adam and Eve is the blueprint of every single sin of every person in all of human history. Listen closely to your experience and you will be able to trace the three parts of *listening with new ears, seeing differently,* and *acting to experiment* in your particular sins. First comes interior disobedience, then new desires followed by lusts. And in the action to satisfy the lust, we take what does not belong to us—what we really don't need—violating poverty.

But how do we account for the excitement that accompanies sinful acts? Doesn't the excitement indicate we are on to some positive human good? There is a genuine excitement in becoming the center of my own universe—of stepping out into the "new" experiences of life. Not unlike the prodigal son who was lured by the promise of leaving his home and experimenting in a foreign land.

However, if you listen closely to your heart, you will feel both excitement *and* fear commingled in sinful contemplation and experimentation. The rush of excitement tinged with fear in sinful acts is a combination of becoming your "own god," and yet consciously or unconsciously knowing that you are violating the very commandments of the One, True God. It is impossible to contemplate sinful actions or to sin and not feel fear and anxiety. This is so because sin at its core severs our hearts and wills from God. Such actions for those made in God's image must by their very nature engender fear and trembling.

That one small action of Adam and Eve, seemingly so insignificant, leads to the fratricide of Cain and Abel, to the collapse of the Tower of Babel, and to the history of evil, with which we are so familiar. One sinful experiment can lead to another and another till a person, a people, a race, a nation, are more and more cut off from God's life and mission. Both the individual and the corporate conscience are darkened, no longer seeing distinctions between good and evil. The mission to serve self seems more real and attractive—a greater positive human good—than to be obedient to the voice of God in our hearts. It becomes very hard even to hear God's voice in our hearts.

The legacy of the divided human heart and the rejection of God's mission and plan for humankind and the world are manifest throughout all of human history. It is even manifest in the human members of the church. Our sinfulness harms the body of Christ and the church, marring the unity that God desires. God will prevail however, even over the sinfulness of Christians, because Jesus' passion, death, and resurrection have forever broken the tragic legacy of sin.

Listen to how sin works in your life. Try to trace the threefold patterns of listening, seeing, and acting—disobedience, lust, and greed. How are you tempted to be your own god? What issues and choices most appeal to your ego so that making your *own* decisions over and above God's authority gives you a sense of being your *own* person.

You may be helped to think of sin as a tree with roots, a trunk, branches, and fruit. See your individual sins as fruit on a tree. Tracing back from the fruit to the branches to the trunk to the roots, pray for the grace to understand the *root* sins in your life. While all sinful fruit manifests characteristics of the seven capital sins (pride, anger, envy, greed, lust, avarice, laziness), the *trunk* and *root* sin in our lives will most likely be localized in one or other of these—pride is almost always present because the first sin appealed to human pride and independence from God.

Coming Home—the Joy of Reconciliation

The prodigal son came home to satisfy his most basic needs for food. Perhaps in expecting to be treated at best as hired help, he had given up hope of having the love and friendship that makes a real home. After all, he betrayed his father, his family name, his people, and his religion. But Jesus clearly intends us to understand the father's response to the lost son as God's response to all sinners who are lost and seek reconciliation. We expect to be punished in some way because of our violations. But in the father's response, Jesus portrays a love and mercy that knows no limits, even in the face of sinfulness that knew no limits. Far from being punished, the father celebrates and gives the boy a signet ring symbolizing his reinstatement as a son with all family privileges.

The sacrament of reconciliation is the pathway back home to paradise and to the active participation in God's mission. For this reason, it is a prayer of joy and a real missionary activity. The more profoundly we are in touch with our sinfulness, the deeper our joy becomes when we surrender our sin and weakness to Jesus and surrender anew to his mission and kingdom. In reconciliation we are, through the power and mercy of God, reclaiming our lost home, our original mission, and the paradise of peace and joy God always intended us to share.

St. Ignatius considers it a grace to know our sinfulness, for in knowing it, we come to realize that we need Jesus as Redeemer. It is the Tempter that makes us feel we cannot go home or that we won't be forgiven. Never forget the lessons of the prodigal son. God will never turn you away, no matter your sins. If you feel fear, realize it is coming from the one who wants you to lose hope in ever being able to go home or to start over. Fear and loss of hope play big parts in the Tempter's *strategy* to keep us "lost" and tethered to his mission.

The Joy of Reconciliation Is Both Yours and Jesus'

Jesus died to save you *from* eternal loss and *for* eternal life and to reclaim human history and creation for the Creator. He did this out of love for you. I believe that Jesus would have suffered and died to save just one lost soul, he loves us individually that much. Give Jesus the joy of knowing that his sacrifice for you is bearing fruit. Give him the joy of confessing your sinfulness and letting him forgive you and start you once again on the mission that gives your life meaning and hope. You can give Jesus, the Good Shepherd, no greater gift. He loves us in our weakness and sinfulness and *never* judges harshly the one who genuinely seeks his forgiveness.

Before Christ's atoning death, *no one* had the hope of eternal life with God. Jesus' death has won our reconciliation. When we express sorrow for our sinfulness and seek God's forgiveness, we are healed and grow in the perfection won for us by Christ. In confessing and being pardoned, we have the sure hope of gaining eternal life. Nothing can bring us more joy. Nothing can bring Jesus more joy than our taking seriously his ultimate gift of reconciling love.

I consider the reception of the sacrament of reconciliation on a regular basis an incredible way to deepen my relationship with God and to strengthen me on my own mission for God's kingdom. For this reason, I think of it not just as a pathway to God but as an important form of prayer. I also know that frequent reception has significantly increased my joy, happiness, and peace.

The Second Vatican Council calls the sacrament of reconciliation the second most important means toward growth in holiness. The first is the Eucharist. Since the church is in the business of producing a holy, missionary people for the purpose of transforming the world in the image of Christ, it is no wonder she would be interested in promoting this gift of healing and joy. John Paul II, in his address for the World Day of Peace for 2002, said that there is no peace in the world without justice and no justice without forgiveness. The personal path toward that peace, justice, and forgiveness of which he speaks begins for each Catholic in this great sacrament of healing. Barring serious sin, we are asked to receive this sacrament only once a year. I am constantly amazed at how little is asked of us in our faith commitment. You may want to consider a frequency that is closer to once a month. I think the Holy Father goes daily. Frequent reception on a monthly basis will do more than you can possibly imagine in helping you grow in faith and closeness to God and in self-awareness of your own mission in life.

The subjects in the three categories mentioned below are ways we can fall into temptation and follow the mission of the Tempter. These different categories are helpful reflections to keep us alert to God's mission and where we often need Jesus' reconciling love to get back on track in our lives. Take your time in praying over your life. Pray to understand the patterns of temptation to which you are susceptible. Pray to God to know where you need the forgiveness of Jesus. Know that you are moving more deeply toward your true mission in life. Your efforts to grow in this way bring joy not only to your heart but also to Jesus'. Make the sacrament of reconciliation a regular part of the mission of your spiritual life.

In My Relationship with God...

- Do I take the time to make this relationship one that is real and vital, with a life of prayer and thanksgiving?

- Have I considered religious preoccupations foolish, peripheral, or of no consequence in my life?
- Do I skip Sunday Mass for the sake of convenience? Am I aware that to do so is a grave sin?
- Do I receive the Lord in communion without going to confession when I have consciously committed some grave sin like missing Mass on Sunday or a holy day or engaging in sexual intercourse outside of marriage?
- Do I regularly doubt God's love for other people or myself?
- Do I receive the sacrament of reconciliation at least once a year to gain the grace of forgiveness?
- Do I make up my own rules for right and wrong, and discard the teachings of the Gospel and the church when they begin to press upon my own life?
- Do I profane God's holy name by using Jesus or God as a swear word?

In Relationship to My Own Life...

- Do I live for ease and comfort?
- Have I lacked gratitude for the basic blessings of life, health, and friends?
- Do I allow power or money to control my plans and relationships? This is idolatry, worshiping a god other than God.
- Have I failed to cultivate my natural talents?
- Have I abused my body and/or health?
- Do I abuse alcohol or drugs?

- Do I use or purchase pornography from magazines, movies or off the Internet?
- Do I speak up about my beliefs and convictions in appropriate ways in public settings, or do I let my fear of rejection silence me?
- Do I rationalize sinful behavior instead of allowing myself to be challenged to face the responsibility of my actions?
- Have I had an abortion?

In My Relationships with Others...

- Do I treat my parents, family and friends with respect and love?
- Have I rejected the love or friendship of another?
- Have I failed to share what I am able to share in goods or services with the poor and needy?
- Have I harmed another's reputation by gossip or malicious talk?
- Have I failed to forgive certain people?
- Do I hold onto anger? Am I envious of others?
- Do I hold sacred and reserve sexual intimacy for marriage? (This is not a law made up by the church, but a command of Christ himself that the church has a responsibility to proclaim as Jesus' Way, Truth and Life.)
- Have I assisted another in getting an abortion?
- Have I tried to control others for my own personal satisfaction or have I been cruel, hateful, or self-centered in dealing with individuals or groups?

- Have I been faithful to friends who need my help or support?
- Am I truthful in my use of money and in business? Have I lied? Have I cheated on exams or papers?
- Have I stolen money or possessions from others?

Pattern of Individual Reconciliation

The priest usually begins with the sign of the cross and then says a short prayer, inviting the Spirit of the Father to be present to you as you confess your sins. Tell the priest when you last received the sacrament of reconciliation and then confess the matters that you have on your mind and in your heart. While speaking your sins out loud, you are actually speaking them to the Father in the presence of the priest, who stands in God's stead as a representative of Christ's church and ambassador for God.

The priest will give you a few words of encouragement and then offer you a penance. He will then ask you to turn to God, using a prayer to ask God for forgiveness. You may use one of the following prayers or you may make one up.

My God,
I am sorry for my sins with all my heart.
In choosing to do wrong
and failing to do good,
I have sinned against you
whom I should love above all things.
I firmly intend, with your help,
to do penance, to sin no more,

and to avoid whatever leads me to sin.
Our Savior Jesus Christ
suffered and died for us.
In His name, my God, have mercy.

Or:

Wash me from my guilt
and cleanse me of my sin.
I acknowledge my offense;
my sin is before me always.

Or:

Remember, Lord, your compassion and mercy that you
showed long ago.
Do not recall the sins and failings of my youth.
In your mercy remember me, Lord, because of your goodness.

Or:

Father, I desire to be part of Jesus' mission in the world.
Forgive me the ways that I have turned from that mission
and wash me clean of all the sins in my life that I confessed
today. I know by your grace I can do all things, because the
Lord Jesus has conquered the powers of darkness. I ask Jesus
to strengthen me to share his mission and to send his Spirit to
enlighten me. In his name, I pray. Amen.

After your prayer, the priest will give you sacramental absolution. He may lay his hands on your head as he prays,

invoking the Spirit of God to give you peace and forgiveness.
He will say the following beautiful prayer:

> *God the Father of mercies*
> *through the death and resurrection of His Son*
> *has reconciled the world to Himself*
> *and sent the Holy Spirit among us*
> *for the forgiveness of sins;*
> *through the ministry of the Church*
> *may God give you pardon and peace,*
> *and I absolve you from your sins*
> *in the name of the Father, and the Son,*
> *and of the Holy Spirit.*

You respond: *Amen.*

5

Praying with the Scriptures

Using the Old and New Testaments for prayer enables you to open your spirit to the inspired word of God and allows that word to speak anew to your heart each day. The stories of the Old Testament, the Psalms, the Gospels, and the apostolic letters are powerful sources of inspiration, consolation, instruction, and hope. They have been given to us for this very purpose and to help us understand our mission in life. The following pattern of praying with the Scriptures has been adapted from Father Armand Nigro, S.J., and is a wonderful way or method for allowing the Spirit to open you to the word of God.[1]

Gods Speaks to Us First

God is concerned for each of us and wants to communicate with us:

- through Jesus, the Word of God
- through the church, the extension of Jesus in the world
- through others, because we are joined together in Jesus

---

1. Father Nigro's materials are not copyrighted and he wants them freely shared with all God's people.

- through visible creation around us, the physical context of our lives (creation is through Jesus and is God's
revelation)
- through the events of our lives
- through the Holy Scripture, a real form of God's
presence

God Invites Us to Listen

Our response to God's initiative is to listen to what is
said. This is a basic attitude of prayer. Here is a way to go
about listening:

- What one does immediately before prayer is important.
- Quiet yourself and relax in a prayerful, comfortable
position. When we listen to someone, we try to give
the person undivided attention. Search for silence and
solitude. Remember that Jesus would often go off by
himself to pray to the Father.
- Select a passage of Scripture.
The fewer verses, the better. Put a marker in the page.
- Be conscious of your experiences: feelings, thoughts,
hopes, loving, wondering, desiring.
- Be conscious of God's unselfish, unconditional, loving
presence in you; acknowledge this simply by saying
something like this from your heart: "You love me,
you are present to me, you live in me." Ask for the
grace to listen.
- Begin to read the Scripture slowly, attentively. Do not
try and hurry to cover all the material. If the passage

recounts an event in Jesus' life, be there. Share with the persons who are in the scene. Respond to what Jesus is saying. It is meant for you.

- Some words and phrases carry special meaning for you. Savor them and turn them over in your heart. If you read or recite a psalm or other prayer from Scripture, mean what you are saying and make it your own.
- When something strikes you, PAUSE.

  These may be times when God is speaking directly to you. Do not hurry to move on. Wait until you are no longer moved by the experience. That something may be when:

  —you feel a new way of being with Jesus, such as what it means to be healed by him; you experience God's love;

  —you feel lifted in your spirit;

  —you are inspired to do something good;

  —you are happy and content just to be in God's presence;

  —you feel disturbed, puzzled, or even repelled by something in Scripture.

Do not get discouraged if nothing seems to happen. Sometimes God lets us feel dry and empty in order to let us realize it is not within our power to communicate with God or to experience consolation. Only God can give us a sense of the Spirit's presence and the gift of consolation. God is always very close to you even in seeming absence (cf. Ps 139:7–9).

Remember Paul's words: *Likewise the Spirit helps us in our weakness for we do not know how to pray as we ought, but that very Spirit intercedes with sighs too deep for words. And God, who searches the heart, knows what is the mind of the Spirit, because the Spirit intercedes for the saints according to the will of God* (Rom 8:26–27).

Relax in prayer. God will "speak to you."

> *For as the rain and the snow come down from heaven,*
> *and do not return there until they have watered the earth,*
> *making it bring forth and sprout,*
> *giving seed to the sower and bread to the eater,*
> *so shall my word be that goes forth from my mouth;*
> *it shall not return to me empty,*
> *but it shall accomplish that which I purpose,*
> *and succeed in the thing for which I sent it.*

(Isa 55:10–11)

Just be conscious that God is present all around you. Try simply to be there, and let God love you and you love God.

Summary: The Five "P"s

PLACE—where you are alone and uninhibited in God's presence.

PICK a passage from Scripture. Have it marked and ready.

POSTURE—stay relaxed and peaceful, in harmony of body and spirit.

PRESENCE—of God. Be aware of it, acknowledge it, and respond to it even if you "feel nothing."

PRAY the passage. Read it very slowly aloud. Listen carefully, peacefully to it.

Conclusion

Do not be anxious or try to look for implications, lessons, profound thoughts, conclusions, or resolutions. Be content, like a child who climbs into Mom or Dad's lap and listens to a story. When you finish, remind yourself that God continues to live in you the rest of the day and forever.

6.

Discerning God's Voice

In the last discourse in John's Gospel, Jesus tells his disciples that if they love him they will keep his commandments and he will pray to his Father to send them another Counselor to be with them forever. Jesus calls the Counselor the "Spirit of truth." Jesus speaks about the promise of the gift of the Spirit in connection with the living of the commandments (John 14:15–17). God will not leave us orphaned when we are struggling to live rightly, but gives us the Spirit as our guide to help us discern the way of truth in all the choices and decisions of our lives.

St. Ignatius was given the great gift of discerning the spirits. He was aware that someone making a retreat and consciously trying to open their hearts to the will of God and God's mission in the world would experience a movement of different spirits. Ignatius's method involved becoming attuned to discerning the different voices or spirits in our lives.

There are three such voices or spirits present in our lives: God's Spirit, our own ego, and the evil spirit or as he is called in the Scriptures, the prince of this world. At all times of the day we are being influenced and tugged at by any or all of these spirits. Learning to listen to our hearts to know how the different voices "sound" is one of the most important ways of praying because it helps us to discern truth from falsehood and to grow in genuine freedom to follow our true mission in life.

Ignatius learned that the Holy Spirit and the evil spirit each have signature characteristics and the two principle spiritual realities we experience in relation to them are called spiritual *consolations* and spiritual *desolations.* These spiritual realities are the direct result of both the Holy Spirit and the Tempter or the evil spirit (Ignatius calls him the *enemy of our human nature*) acting upon our soul.

Ignatius wrote his rules for discernment for those making a retreat. But what holds true for retreatants also holds true for the one who tries to live a Christian life day to day. Both the Holy Spirit and the Tempter are constantly acting upon us, as I mentioned above. So is the force of our own ego. Talk of an "evil spirit" might sound a little old-fashioned in the modern age, but it is a truth of our faith that a personal evil power exists. The Second Vatican Council speaks seventeen times of this evil, using words like "Satan," "evil one," "ancient serpent," "devil," "prince of this world," and "powers of darkness." What many consider the most positive and optimistic document of the Council, *Gaudium et Spes,* speaks five times of this personal, evil force. I have tried to detail his strategies in section 4 above.

In fact, Jesus died doing battle with the powers of darkness. Recall that during the great Easter Vigil and Easter Sunday, the holiest celebrations of the entire liturgical year, we renew our baptismal promises. In the renewal, we are asked to reject Satan and all his powers, glamor, and empty promises. *And* we are asked to profess faith in God the Father, Jesus the Redeemer, the Holy Spirit, the church, the communion of saints, the forgiveness of sin, the resurrection of the body, and life everlasting. The formula for our baptismal vows details the two global realities and the two missions—darkness and light. The struggle for light over darkness is the essence of Christian life. You are asked to *reject* the mission of darkness and to *accept* the mission of light. It sounds a bit like the film *Star Wars*, but it is true. In fact, this is why I mentioned in the foreword that *Star Wars* and movies of similar genre, like the *Lord of the Rings*, are so successful. They tap into our unconscious understanding of the reality of the battle between good and evil in the universe. In a world that has deconstructed the supernatural realms of both the holy and the wicked, we find hidden meaning in cinematic mythology that express the religious realities that we all know are true but can no longer express directly.

Perhaps the greatest single barrier to discerning these different voices is the noise in the world. We rarely allow ourselves a moment's quiet. How often are you quiet with your heart turned to God? *"Be still, and know that I am God"* (Ps 46:10). The evil spirit can rule supreme in the noise, because your capacity to see, hear, or feel what is going on in your heart is *greatly* diminished in the distractions and noise of life.

Learning the art of spiritual discernment requires that you understand the experiences of both spiritual consolation and spiritual desolation. The effect of the experiences of consolation and desolation can be powerful *or* subtle. What are the trademark qualities of spiritual consolation and desolation?

Spiritual Consolation

Spiritual consolation is a grace and gift from God. It is different from just feeling good or being happy. It is a spiritual reality and not a psychological state, although it can be psychologically uplifting. *One or more of the following qualities define spiritual consolations:*

- When I have a feeling of love for God or of Jesus that makes me love all other aspects of life and creation precisely because of my love for God.
- When motivated by a love of God, I cry because of sorrow for my sins or because of the suffering that Jesus endured for me or, if I cry for another reason, and it moves me to have a deeper love and understanding of God.
- When I have an experience that increases or deepens in me faith in God, hope in God, or love of God.
- When I have an experience of joy and find myself attracted to spiritual things that lead me to want to commit my life to the things of heaven, the values of the Gospel, and the salvation of my soul.
- When I find myself peaceful and quiet in an experience of God's presence. This "presence" is when I know intellectually and/or in my heart and emotions that I am not alone. The feelings of peace and quiet are directly connected to the presence of God made manifest to me.

Spend some time reflecting upon your life in the experiences of spiritual consolation listed above. Based on the descriptive definitions listed, try to identify some particular experience of spiritual consolation that has happened recently. It could be very simple or very profound. What was it? When did it happen? What did you experience? Was it a new experience or one that you can remember having before at some other time in your life? How has this type of spiritual consolation affected your practice of faith, prayer, and your participation in the Eucharist and the sacrament of reconciliation? How has it affected your consideration of your future vocation or career—your mission in life?

Realize that these consolations are graces and gifts from God. What might God be "telling" you in light of it? (For example, if you went to confession recently and felt happy and joyful after the experience, that was a consolation from God. It could be saying: "You don't need to fear, I will always love and forgive you. Keep trying to do your best but always trust in my love when you fail." It could also be saying: "Remember how much you feared coming to confession for fear of being judged harshly? All I want for you is peace and joy, and for you to realize that the one who makes you fearful is not me but the one who wants to destroy your peace and hope. Don't pay attention to the voice of fear in the future because he is a spirit of falsehood.")

Spiritual Desolation

Spiritual desolation characterizes a spiritual state of soul. God permits us to experience desolation when we turn away from the Lord and the practice of our faith. God also permits spiritual desolation to teach us something important about ourselves in relation to God's power and majesty. Spiritual desolation is different from emotional depression. One can be emotionally depressed but still have an inner calm and peace and an awareness of God and thus be in a state of spiritual consolation. What, then, is spiritual desolation? It can be characterized by the following:

- Spiritual desolation is entirely the opposite of spiritual consolation.
- Your spirit feels dark and in turmoil.
- You feel more attracted or drawn by things that are of the earthly, material world than of the spiritual realm.
- You feel restlessness, disturbances, and temptations that create in you a lack of faith in God, hope, and love. You doubt the reality of God or the positive experiences you had in a time of spiritual consolation.
- Your spirit feels lazy or lukewarm. The spiritual fire and energy is gone.
- Your spirit is sad and you feel separated from God as if a spiritual hole has opened in your soul.
- All the thoughts and inspirations you felt in the spiritual consolation are replaced by their opposite in this time of spiritual desolation. You feel impatient or frustrated or annoyed by spiritual realities and positive moral values.
- You feel that a commitment to spiritual practices is a waste of time, or if you are still doing them, you feel you are getting little, if anything, from your efforts.

Spend some time reflecting on your life in the context of the above definition of spiritual desolation. Try to identify a period of time when, according to the definition above, you were in a state of spiritual desolation. What was happening in your life? What was the experience of desolation like? What types of thoughts did you have about God and faith during this time? Have you had these experiences often in your life? Can you remember another time when you felt this way? To what do you attribute these feelings? How has this type of spiritual desolation affected your practice of faith, prayer, participation in the Eucharist and the sacrament of reconciliation? How has it affected your consideration of your future vocation or career—your mission in life?

Making Decisions Using Spiritual Discernment

Decisions large and small can be made using the knowledge gained from understanding the workings of consolation and desolation in your life. I will share with you a major decision I made over an important apostolic choice using my knowledge of consolation and desolation.

Once, I had to make a choice between two courses of action, both of which were good uses of my talents, and my superior approved of both of them. It was an important decision that would impact my life for at least ten years. One of the options created in me an intense excitement that the other failed to generate. I was "naturally" drawn to the one that excited me. On the other hand, I did not feel a great sense of peacefulness when I thought about it. Excitement and peace don't always go hand in hand, I discovered. The other less exciting option, when I thought about it, created in me a great calm and peace. The option with greater allure and excitement pressed upon me, and I really wanted to choose it. However, I did not feel the sense of peaceful consolation that I knew was a sign of a good discernment. I waited for three months (fortunately, I had the time to delay a decision) while I struggled with the peacefulness the other option created. Yes, I struggled with the peacefulness! My head told me the exciting option was the "better" option, but my "heart" was telling me the other course of action was where God was present. I wanted the exciting option. What was going on here?

In listening more deeply, the exciting option had many traits of spiritual desolation. Underneath the excitement I sensed very little "increase in faith, hope, and love," but I did realize that this option appealed to many ego desires. On one level, it made me feel more important in ways I wanted to be important. It appealed to my desire to get ahead. It gave me a greater sense of status and serving my own image. This was hard for me to admit to myself. And since both options had been approved by my superior, I had to be very honest with myself and what my heart, in my knowledge of spiritual discernment, was telling me. I had to admit that I wanted the option that made me feel more important, not the one that was giving me a sense of peace. If I did not take the time to step back and listen honestly and deeply to my heart, it would have been easy to confuse "feeling more important" with "peace and security."

This is not to say that God cannot work though my bad choices. God is working constantly to bring me to the light of freedom, even through bad choices. God did not want the

Israelites to choose kings to rule them and warned them that it was not God's design for the Chosen People. They rejected God's voice, but God continued to work through the decision they made for the ultimate good God planned for them.

Even if I had chosen the option that did not bring me the consolation that is a sign of God's presence, the Lord would have taken my bad choice and sought to lead me to the point of freedom and peace achievable within that situation. People striving to do God's will often find themselves choosing between two goods, not between good and evil. But God knows better than I the option that will more readily move me in the direction of the true peace, freedom, and hope I desire. To move in the opposite directions means delaying the gifts God has in store for me. It can also mean a diminishment of the ultimate good I am capable of doing to serve him in the work of the kingdom.

In listening for God's voice in decision making, we must learn that God wants to lead us to what will bring us genuine hope and peace in following our mission in life *and,* at the same time, what serves God's kingdom and our mission to help bring that about. Contemplating the "exciting" option was not bringing me the peace I knew I needed to make an honest "discernment." On top of that, I realized that it was not God's kingdom I desired to serve in contemplating it, but my own sense of worldly success.

The option that gave me a constant sense of calm had none of the immediate allure, but I knew it was the right one. The peace I received in thinking about it was like God telling me: "Trust your heart, I will be present in this course of action, and it is the one that will lead you to your deeper desires. This will carry you further on your mission. You can't see it now, but I want you to trust me that the peace you are feeling is a sign of my Spirit leading you."

Our hearts are often confused and divided due to human weakness and sinfulness. If we desire to make choices that are centered in God, we need to listen to the information that God gives us in the movements of consolation and desolation. Learning to listen to the different movements or voices takes some time. A good retreat experience can lead you to the initial knowledge of how these two spiritual realities "feel" in your own life. You might also consider asking a spiritual director to help you listen more deeply to the spirits working inside of you, especially if you want to make a major decision in the light of God's grace. As I said at the start of this reflection, it is important to know that every moment of every day, spiritual powers are acting on your heart and mind to move you in different directions and for the purpose of two distinct missions. It is important to take the time to learn the signature characteristics of the Spirit of God and the enemy of your human nature. In this way, being fully awake to the spiritual realm in your life, your choices will more and more reflect a life grounded in the power of light and freedom. You will also come to recognize more clearly the mission you are to play at the side of Christ the King in advancing his kingdom of truth, justice, love, and peace.

Once you learn the difference between the various spirits working in your life, here are three very basic but very important pieces of advice on discernment, two from St. Ignatius and a third from St. Paul:

- First, absolutely *never* make an important life decision when you are in a state of spiritual desolation. The data will always be flawed, and you will never be able to discern well or choose rightly. Remember the author of the desolation is the one we call the "Father of Lies." Make major decisions only in times of consolation, but not *hurriedly*. Test the decision, speak with a spiritual advisor or confessor, and only act when the decision is confirmed by further consolation.

- Second, Ignatius would also remind you that if you are in a state of consolation, give thanks to God for the graces you are receiving from the consolation. And if you are in consolation, prepare yourself spiritually to survive a time of desolation that is sure to follow. Should you find yourself in a time of desolation and feel that you can't survive much longer, remember that consolation is soon to come. Be patient and ask for God's help. You may feel that the Lord will never arrive but God never, absolutely never leaves you alone. Remember the prayer "Footprints." It is in part 3 if you have forgotten it.

- Third, those who place their trust in Jesus have nothing to fear from the evil one. The evil one can only have power over us if we freely and consciously submit to him. Jesus has conquered the powers of death and darkness, and we will have victory in Christ if we surrender our lives to him. Are you are striving to be a good Christian but find that you are living with an anxious fear of the evil one? Then you are in a state of desolation and you should pray for consolation to return. God is always at your side, why should you be afraid?

For I am convinced that neither death, nor life, nor angels, nor rulers, nor things present, nor things to come, nor powers, nor height, nor depth, nor anything else in all creation, will be able to separate us from the love of God in Christ Jesus our Lord. (Rom 8:38–39)

Part Two

Pray Always:
Awareness of God throughout the Day

Sometimes people get upset when I tell them that God does not need our prayers. God is complete perfection and was completely satisfied even before humankind was created. So then, why pray? We pray because we *need* to pray to become aware of God's presence in our lives and to call upon his aid and mercy to follow our true mission in life. God wants to help us and chances are we won't remember that fact or ask for the help if we forget about God. Prayer helps us, not God.

St. Paul says: *"Rejoice always, pray without ceasing, give thanks in all circumstances; for this is the will of God in Christ Jesus for you. Do not quench the Spirit"* (1 Thess 5:16–19). Because we are embodied spirits, we need simple reminders of God's presence in our lives so that we don't *quench the Spirit* who seeks constantly to help us.

Consider the following suggestions in this section as simple pathways to become more aware of God during the day. They are ways of praying and aids to prayer and holiness that have been used by countless millions of Christians throughout the ages. In your attempt to "pray constantly," you will ask God more frequently for grace and assistance. You will also become more conscious of how God is protecting, encouraging, consoling, strengthening, and standing with you every moment of every day. This knowledge will bring you enduring peace.

Imagination in Prayer

God is real. Do simple things to bring this fact to life. When you pray, place an empty chair next to you and realize that God is sitting there. Reach out your hands to God when you pray. Kneel at certain times to feel yourself a child before God. Genuflect when you are in the presence of the Blessed Sacrament in a church so that your spirit can honor Christ before you. Rest your head on the shoulder of Christ when you pray or imagine that you are sitting in the lap of Jesus. Extend your hand to your guardian angel when you pray. Close your eyes and see in your mind's eye the Lord helping you. Embrace Christ on the cross by holding a crucifix when you pray. When you go for walks or out for exercise or for a run, ask the Lord to be with you and offer your exercise for a particular need or grace for yourself, the church, friends and family, or the world. Use your imagination in all sorts of ways to help you pray.

On Forgiving, Loving, and Serving Others

One of the best ways to be conscious of God in the course of your day is through the people you meet. God loves every single person. You are called to love them as Christ loves them. The fact of the matter is that some anger you, others bore you, others have hurt you, some you envy, some you treat as objects for your pleasure or personal gain, some need your help, and some are just good friends who are a source of joy and support. Treat each of these people as Christ would treat them. How will you become aware of God doing this? The task of loving, forgiving, and serving each of these individuals as Christ has asked you is something only God's grace can accomplish in you. In your efforts to love as Jesus did, you will have to call upon God for help because you won't have the strength to do it on your own. Thus, you will be calling upon the Lord quite often during the day as you strive to serve him better in all the people you meet.

When you see someone you are not getting along with, in your heart, ask Jesus to help you love him or her like he does. When you encounter a friend, in your heart, thank God for the friendship. If you find yourself judging some person or group of people, ask God to be merciful to yourself and not judge you as you have judged others. If you find yourself lusting after someone or using some person for your own ends, ask in your heart for forgiveness and the ability to see the person as God sees them. If you see someone who needs your help and you feel unable to offer it at that time, ask God to help the person. When you encounter tragedies and human suffering you feel helpless to solve, ask God to help solve them. In the morning, ask God to help you know, of all the people who cross your path that day, the ones you can help. Every person needs your Christlike response, and if you give it in this simple way, your life will be transformed by the power of Christ working in you.

Praying for Your Family

Nothing has had more influence on your life and personality than your family: Mom and Dad, brothers and sisters, and grandparents. Often our greatest joys *and* sufferings are connected with our family relationships. We can take the graces and love from our family relationships for granted; often forgetting the great love and sacrifices given on our behalf, especially from our parents. Also, in the face of our parents' both real and imagined imperfections and the very real problems that might be present in our family, we can easily justify our angers and resentments, sometimes holding these resentments in our hearts for years.

No matter how good or bad your relationship with your family, you owe them your prayers, especially your mom and dad. You will gain grace and strength by praying for your family in both good and difficult times. You gain nothing and only hurt yourself when you cut your family out of your thoughts and prayers or hold anger and resentments in your heart.

Connect some daily ritual (taking a shower, making your bed, shaving, driving to work, preparing to exercise, etc.) with a simple prayer for the members of your family. Ask God to be with them, giving them what they need that day, and mention each of them by name to God. This should take you only a matter of seconds, but its long-term effects in assisting those closest to you and transforming your heart is of incomparable value.

Grace before Meals

Say a short thanksgiving before you eat. Do this even if you are out at a restaurant. It you feel it inappropriate to pray out loud or make the sign of the cross, pause and quietly recognize the blessing of food that is before you. Remember those who are hungry and ask God to help them. In doing this, you will become more aware that everything you have, even the food you eat, comes from the hand of God.

Taking a Shower and Other Gifts

Have you ever paused to realize how incredible it is to be able to have enough of both water and electricity to take a hot shower any time you want? Most of the people in the world don't have this luxury. Give thanks to God for a wonderful luxury that many people in the world never experience. How many other things are present in daily life that can remind you of how much God has blessed you? Thank God quietly each time you remember something. Soon you will be much more aware of God's constant presence. You will grow in gratitude for so many gifts.

At Noontime

Praying the Angelus at noon is an ancient church tradition. The Angelus (part 3) begins with the lines: "The angel of the Lord declared unto Mary. And she conceived by the Holy Spirit." Pause in your heart wherever you may be at noontime and give thanks for Mary's yes to God. Because of her yes, we have Jesus as Savior. Think how remarkable it was for God to allow the salvation of the human race to depend on the free choice of a mortal human. Think how much God wants to entrust to *you*. All God needs is your cooperation and your *yes* each day.

Pray the Angelus at noon. If you have the time, and a church or chapel is close by, stop by for five minutes and place yourself in the presence of God in the Blessed Sacrament. Ask God to give you the grace to respond with a yes to his call in your own life. Understand that the Lord wants you to share his work and mission in the world. As Mary was open to God's design, pray to be open to God's plan for you to share in his mission.

Three O'Clock Thanksgiving

At three o'clock each day, stop for *a few seconds* and recall that at this hour, Jesus performed the greatest act of love for you and won your freedom from sin and your hope of eternal life. Ask for anything you need from Jesus at this time of day or give a simple thanks to him for this gift or for anything else that crosses your heart and mind. The Lord told St. Faustina that: "In this hour I will refuse nothing to the soul that makes a request of me in virtue of My Passion."[2]

At Times of Temptation and Failure Consciously Turn to God

When we feel tempted or when we experience the failure of sin in our lives, many of us flee from God. But these are the times when we *most need* to bring ourselves before God. In temptation and sin turn your heart immediately to God and ask for help. You are a child of God and will not be turned away. When a little child turns to Mom or Dad looking for help and forgiveness after breaking something or doing something wrong, parents' hearts melt. They lift their son or daughter and hold them close. Jesus is not angry with us when we are tempted or fail. He wants to be with us more than ever during these times because he knows this is when we most need him. Make a conscious effort to let God "see" you in times of temptation and failure. Call upon Jesus for help. Jesus is the Divine Physician. He is most himself when caring for you in times of you pain, failures, and trials.

An Entire Community at Your Service

One way to keep an awareness of God's presence in your life is to call upon the help of those whom the church declared

2. *St. Faustina's Diary*, #59.

to have attained the fullness of life. This is the communion of saints. We are all part of one body in Christ, but those who fully share Christ's love have been given a special role, by virtue of Christ's power and holiness, to aid those of us still struggling to reach our final home.

Here is an idea. Research the saints whose feasts mark important milestones in your life and faith: (birthday, baptismal day, first communion, confirmation, marriage, etc.). Get to know what they did and call upon their help. Ask them to be your patrons on your way to the kingdom. Ask them to work for you, just as you would network with people on earth to help find your mission and to stay faithful to it. Be inspired by their lives and realize that God desires to make you a saint too. Pick a saint as your main patron. I have St. Francis of Assisi because he is the one I chose as my confirmation saint. Because I chose him as my name saint at the time of my adult acceptance of my Catholic faith, I feel he has a special care for me. I offer a prayer to him each morning to help me that day live more in Christ and for his mission. The saints were the ones who lived life to the full. In your efforts to be constantly aware of God, you are also striving to live life to the fullest and win the prize of eternity they now enjoy. St. Thérèse of Lisieux said that she wanted to spend her eternity doing good on earth. God wants us to call upon their help. Take advantage of this great gift of grace.

A Personal Escort

You may think angels are kid stuff, but these noncorporeal, spiritual beings are a truth of our Catholic faith. The new

Catholic catechism says that "as purely *spiritual* creatures, angels have intelligence and will; they are personal and immortal creatures, surpassing in perfection all visible creatures, as the splendor of their glory bears witness."[3] Angels are messengers of God. They have appeared all throughout the Old and New Testaments. An angel announced the birth of Christ, and angels ministered to Jesus at various times in his earthly life. The church teaches that an angel stands beside every believer as a protector and guide. Beings so present in our tradition must have an important function in God's loving plan for each of us.

Pause at the beginning of your day. Ask the angel who guides you to lead you this day: to prepare your way, to defend you against evil and harm, to open you to truth and goodness, to help you see God's gentle hand working in all the people you meet. Ask for help and guidance in all things. When you go to bed at night, ask your angel to stand by you to protect you and to guide your dreams. You will come to know the presence of this powerful friend and protector who will be with you even in paradise. Don't be too sophisticated or overly intellectual to believe in this great helper from God. Remember, Jesus says that unless you change and become like a child, you cannot enter the kingdom of God. Children believe in angels. So should you. They are real and a gift from God to guide you on your mission in life.

---

3. *Catechism of the Catholic Church* (New York: Doubleday, 1995), part 1, #330, p. 96.

Images of God's Mercy and Love

Christians through the ages have used holy images of God the Father, the Holy Spirit, Jesus, the Blessed Mother and the saints to remind them of God's mercy and love. Keep something in your pocket or wallet. Put something in your car. Find a crucifix you like and wear it around your neck. Find one you can place on the wall of your room. Find an image of Christ and of Mary or one of the saints that you like and place it where you can see it in your office, living, study, or work area. We need these physical reminders of the spiritual world and of God's presence in our lives.

Mary and the Rosary

God chose Mary to bring to fruition the plan of eternal salvation. She is rightly called the first Christian. She is a tremendous blessing to us and a powerful advocate for our mission in life to follow more closely in the footsteps of her Son. She was the sacred vessel that brought Christ into the world. God continues to choose Mary as his sacred vessel to bring his message of peace and salvation to the world. The church throughout the centuries has authenticated countless apparitions of Mary. Jesus gave her to us on the cross as our mother, and he wants us to call upon her help. Because of her part in the plan of salvation, the Father, Son, and Holy Spirit always respond to her requests.

St. Catherine of Siena records in her *Dialogues* with the Father that God told her that a particular sinner was preserved from eternal death because of his reverence and love of Mary, the gentle mother of God's only begotten Son. Catherine writes this message from God the Father: "For my goodness, in deference to the Word, has decreed that anyone at all, just or sinner, who holds her [Mary] in due reverence will never be snatched or devoured by the infernal demon. She is like bait set out by my goodness to catch my creatures."[4] The Society of Jesus holds the Blessed Virgin Mary in such high esteem that every Jesuit, by dictate of the order's Constitutions and Complementary Norms, is to consecrate himself to Mary each year on the feast of her Immaculate Heart.

Cardinal Ratzinger has said that the rosary is one of the two deepest and greatest prayers of Christendom (the Stations of the Cross being the second) leading us anew into "the mighty river of the Eucharist. If the Rosary is prayed as tradition envisages, it draws us into a rhythm of calm which makes us flexible and well balanced, giving a name to this peace: Jesus, the blessed fruit of Mary. Mary, who kept the living word in the quiet peace of her heart and was able to become mother of the Incarnate Word. That is why Mary is the ideal of genuine liturgical life. She is Mother of the Church, and as such she also shows us the task and the highest goal of worship: the glory of God, from whom mankind's salvation comes."[5]

---

4. Catherine of Siena, *The Dialogues*, ed. (Mahwah, N.J.: Paulist Press, 1980) Classics of Western Spirituality Series, p. 286.

5. *The Ratzinger Report*: Joseph Cardinal Ratzinger with Vittorio Messori (San Francisco: Ignatius Press, 1985), p. 134.

- You hear the name Mary many times during the day. Turn inward when you hear this name and ask for her help in opening up to God.

- Carry a rosary in your pocket and learn to pray it. It is probably the most widely practiced and highly acclaimed devotional prayer in the history of the church. It is a calming and meditative way to reflect on all the mysteries of the Gospel. Mary will always lead you to Jesus.

- Entrust yourself to Mary's prayers and protection. Consecrate yourself to her yearly on the feast of her Immaculate Heart, the second Saturday after Pentecost.

- Learn how to pray the rosary. The prayers of the rosary are in part 3.

Visit the Lord
in the Blessed Sacrament

Many people live or work close to a church or chapel. The Lord is truly present in the Blessed Sacrament. Go in for a minute or two when you pass by. The church holds this practice in such high esteem that she gives a plenary indulgence (all the temporal punishments due to the effects of your sinful actions are eliminated) to those who give adoration to God for half an hour in the presence of the Blessed Sacrament. The Constitutions of the Jesuit Order also strongly encourage Jesuits daily to frequently visit the Lord in the Blessed Sacrament.

When you visit the Lord in the Blessed Sacrament:

- Genuflect so that your posture helps your spirit honor Christ Jesus in your midst. Ask him to strengthen you for your mission in life. Bring to Christ Jesus all your thoughts and concerns, hopes and joys, fears and hurts. Bring him the cares and anxieties of the world. The grace and strength you will receive from this will transform your day, your life, and your eternity.
- Consecrate yourself to the Sacred Heart of Jesus every year on his feast, the second Friday after Pentecost.

PART THREE

Prayers, Reflections, and Inspirations

The Traditional Morning Offering

O Jesus, through the Immaculate Heart of Mary,
I offer you my prayers, works, joys, sufferings of
*   this day in union with the Holy Sacrifice of the Mass*
*   throughout the world.*
I offer them for all the intentions of your Sacred Heart:
*   the salvation of souls, reparation for sin,*
*   the reunion of all Christians;*

I offer them for the intentions of our bishops,
*   and of the Apostleship of Prayer, and in particular*
*   for those recommended by our Holy Father this month.*

A Morning Offering

O Jesus, I come before you
at the beginning of this day.

I gaze at your face,
I look upon your side
pierced by the lance.

Your wounded heart speaks to me
of God's love poured out of us.

Take, Lord, and receive my heart:
the words of faith that I speak,
the works of justice I would do,
my joys and sufferings.

When I come to the eucharistic table,
gather my offerings to your own
for the life of the world.

At the end of the day,
place me with Mary, your mother,
and for her sake take me to your heart. Amen.

Suscipe

Take, Lord, and receive all my liberty,
my memory, my understanding
and my entire will,
All I have and call my own.

You have given all to me.
To you, Lord, I return it.

Everything is yours. Do with it what you will.
Give me only your love and grace,
That is enough for me.

St. Ignatius Loyola

Prayer for Generosity

Lord, teach me to be generous.
Teach me to serve you as you deserve;
to give and not to count the cost;
to fight and not to heed the wounds;
to toil and not to seek for rest;
to labor and not to ask for reward,
save that knowing that I do your will.

St. Ignatius Loyola

Mediatrix

May it please Our Lady to intercede with her Son
for us poor sinners and obtain this grace for us,

that with the cooperation of our own toil and effort
she may change our weak and sorry spirits and make
them strong and faithful to praise God. Amen.

St. Ignatius Loyola

A Contemplation on the Nativity

This will be to see and consider
what Mary and Joseph are doing,
for example,
making the journey and laboring
that our Lord might be born
in extreme poverty,
and that after many labors,
after hunger, thirst, heat and cold,
after insults and outrages,
He might die on the cross,
and all this for me.

Spiritual Exercises of St. Ignatius

Jesus, King of Nations

Jesus, King of nations and ages, receive the acts of
adoration and praise which we, your children by adoption,
humbly offer to You.

You are the living bread come down from heaven which
gives life to the world. High Priest as well as Victim, You
offered Yourself on the cross in a bloody sacrifice of
expiation to the eternal Father for the redemption of the

human race; and now each day you offer Yourself on our altars by the hands of Your ministers so that there might be restored in each heart Your kingdom of truth and life, of holiness and grace, of justice, love and peace.

King of glory, may Your kingdom come!

Rule from Your throne of glory in the hearts of children so they may keep immaculate the shining purity of their baptismal innocence.

Rule in the hearts of youth so that they may grow in wholesomeness and purity and docility to the voice of those who represent You in the family, school, and Church.

Rule in the heart of the home so that parents and children may live united in the observance of Your holy law.

Rule in our country so that in the harmonious ordering of the social classes all its citizens may regard themselves as children of the same heavenly Father, called to work together for the common temporal good and happy to belong to that one mystical body, of which Your sacrament is both the symbol and the everlasting source.

Rule, finally, King of Kings and Lord of Lords, over all the nations of the earth and enlighten the rulers of each nation that, inspired by Your example, they may nourish thoughts of peace and not of affliction.

Eucharistic Jesus, grant that all people may serve You freely in the knowledge that to serve God is to reign.

May Your Blessed Sacrament, O Jesus, be a light to the mind, strength to the will, and attraction to the heart. May it be a support to the weak, comfort to the suffering, viaticum of salvation to the dying, and for all may it be a pledge of future glory. Amen.

Pope John XXIII

Prayer to Follow Christ

Lord, grant that I may see thee more clearly,
love thee more dearly,
follow thee more nearly.

Spiritual Exercises of St. Ignatius

To Young Adults

All that I can say to you is summed up in the words: Get to know Christ and make yourselves known to Him. He knows each one of you in a particular way...allow Him to find you. A human being, a young person, at times gets lost in himself, in the world about him, and in all the network of human affairs that wrap him 'round. Allow Christ to find you. Let Him know all about you and guide you. It is true that following someone requires also making demands on ourselves. That is the law of friendship. If we wish to travel together, we must pay attention to the road we are to take. If we go walking in the mountains, we must follow the signs. If we go mountain climbing, we cannot let go of the rope. We must also preserve our unity with the Divine Friend whose name is Jesus Christ. We must cooperate with Him.

You are the future of the world, of the nation, of the Church. **Tomorrow depends on you.** *Accept with a sense of responsibility the simple truth contained in this song of youth and ask Christ, through His Mother, that you may be able to face it. Be consistent in your faith. Be faithful to the Mother of Fair Love. Have trust in her, as you shape your love...May Christ always be for you "the way, and the truth, and the life."*

John Paul II

A Prayer to Mary for Human Life

O Mary, bright dawn of the New World,
Mother of the living,
to you do we entrust the **cause of life;**
Look down, O Mother, upon vast numbers
of babies not allowed to be born,
on the poor whose lives are made difficult,
of men and women who are victims of brutal violence,
of the elderly and the sick killed by indifference or
out of misguided mercy.
Grant that all who believe in your Son
may proclaim to the people of our time **the Gospel of life**
with honesty and love.

Obtain for them the grace to **accept that Gospel**
as a gift ever new,
and the joy of **celebrating** *it with gratitude*
throughout their lives and the courage to
bear witness to it *resolutely, in order to build,*
together with all people of good will,
the civilization of truth and love,
to the praise and glory of God,
the Creator and lover of life. Amen.

John Paul II

The Option of Love

Faced with problems and disappointments, many people
    will
try to escape from their responsibility:
escape in selfishness,
escape in sexual pleasure,
escape in drugs,
escape in violence,
escape in indifference and cynical attitudes.
But today, I propose to you
the option of love,
which is the opposite of escape.
If you really accept that love from Christ,
it will lead you to God.
Perhaps in the priesthood or religious life;
perhaps in some special service to your brothers and sisters:
especially the needy, the poor, the abandoned,
those whose rights have been trampled upon,

or those whose basic needs have not been provided for.
Whatever you make of your life,
let it be something that reflects
the love of Christ.
The whole people of God will be the richer
because of the diversity of your commitments.
And whatever you do, remember that
Christ is calling you,
in one way or another,
to the service of love:
the love of God and of your neighbor.

John Paul II ("To Youth," Boston Common, 1979)

Prayer to the Holy Trinity

Eternal Father, confirm me.
Eternal Son, confirm me.
Eternal Holy Spirit, confirm me.
Eternal Trinity confirm me.
My one and only God, confirm me.

St. Ignatius Loyola

The Serenity Prayer

God grant me the serenity to accept the things I cannot
*   change,*
the courage to change the things I can,
and the wisdom to know the difference.

I Asked God...

I asked God for strength,
that I might achieve,
I was made weak,
that I might learn humbly to obey...
I asked for health,
that I might do greater things,
I was given infirmity,
that I might do better things...
I asked for riches,
that I might be happy,
I was given poverty,
that I might be wise...
I asked for power,
that I might have the praise of all,
I was given weakness,
that I might feel the need of God...
I asked for all things that I might enjoy life,
I was given life that I might enjoy all things...
I got nothing that I asked for—
but everything I had hoped for...
Almost despite myself,
my unspoken prayers were answered,
I am among all people
most richly blessed.

Unknown

The Way to Peace

The fruit of silence is prayer.
The fruit of prayer is faith.
The fruit of faith is love.
The fruit of love is service.
The fruit of service is peace.

Mother Teresa

Who Is Jesus to Me?

Jesus is the word made flesh.
Jesus is the bread of life.
Jesus is the victim offered for our sins on the cross.
Jesus is the sacrifice offered at the holy mass for the sins of
the world and mine.

Jesus is the word	*—to be spoken.*
Jesus is the truth	*—to be told.*
Jesus is the way	*—to be walked.*
Jesus is the light	*—to be lit.*
Jesus is the life	*—to be lived.*
Jesus is the love	*—to be loved.*
Jesus is the joy	*—to be shared.*
Jesus is the sacrifice	*—to be offered.*
Jesus is the peace	*—to be given.*
Jesus is the bread of life	*—to be eaten.*
Jesus is the hungry	*—to be fed.*
Jesus is the thirsty	*—to be satiated.*
Jesus is the naked	*—to be clothed.*

Jesus is the homeless —to be taken in.
Jesus is the sick —to be healed.
Jesus is the lonely —to be loved.
Jesus is the unwanted —to be wanted.
Jesus is the leper —to wash his wounds.
Jesus is the beggar —to give him a smile.
Jesus is the drunkard —to listen to him.
Jesus is the little one —to embrace him.
Jesus is the blind —to lead him.
Jesus is the crippled —to walk with him.
Jesus is the dumb —to speak for him.
Jesus is the prisoner —to be visited.
Jesus is the old —to be served.
To me—
Jesus is my God.
Jesus is my life.
Jesus is my spouse.
Jesus is my only love.
Jesus is my all in all.
Jesus is my everything.

Mother Teresa

The Angelus

The angel of the Lord declared unto Mary.
And she conceived by the Holy Spirit.
R. Hail Mary....
Behold the handmaid of the Lord.
Be it done unto me according to your word.

R. *Hail Mary....*
And the word was made flesh;
and dwelt among us.
R. *Hail Mary....*
Pray for us, O holy Mother of God,
that we may be made worthy of the promises of Christ.
Let us pray:
Pour forth we beg you, O Lord,
your grace into our hearts, that we,
to whom the incarnation of Christ, Your Son,
was made known by the message of an angel,
may by his Passion and Cross be brought
to the glory of his resurrection;
Through the same Christ our Lord. Amen.

Footprints

In Heaven, the Lord Jesus reviewed my life with me.
He showed me that He was always with me,
even at the most difficult times in my life.
To prove this, he let me see his footprints walking
next to me at each moment of my life.
I noticed that at the most difficult times in my life,
there was only one set of footprints in the sand.
I asked the Lord why he was not present during
those difficult times as he had promised.
He told me, "My child, when you only see one set
of footprints in those times of trial, it was because
during those moments I was carrying you."

How to Serve God

If you want to serve God,
fall in love and stay in love.

Pedro Arrupe, S.J.

Prayer before a Crucifix

Lord Jesus, what have I done for you?
Lord, Jesus, what am I doing for you?
Lord, Jesus, what will I do for you?

St. Ignatius Loyola

In Times of Suffering

The everlasting God has in his wisdom foreseen from
eternity the cross that he now presents to you as a gift from
his inmost heart. This cross he now sends you, he has
considered with his all-knowing eyes, understood with his
Divine mind, tested with his wise justice, warmed with
loving arms, and weighed with his own hand to see that it
be not one inch too large and not one ounce too heavy for
you. He has blessed it with his holy name, anointed it with
his grace, perfumed it with his consolation, taken one last
glance at you and your courage, and then sent it to you
from heaven, a special greeting from God to you, an alm
of the All-Merciful Love of God.

St. Francis De Sales

His Dream for Me

God created me freely
Out of an overwhelming LOVE I came to be,
He wanted to share his LIFE with me
And hoped I might share my life with him.
He brought me beautiful gifts
And showered me with surprises
So that I might grow in love of him.
So many, many Gifts…
Some to be received in love,
Others to be surrendered in love.
Before his Gifts I shall stand Free
With open hands and heart,
Ready to embrace or to surrender.
For what is essential is not the Gift
But only the Giver—
The Giver who dreams his dream for me.

Unknown

For…

For all that has been—

THANKS!

For all that is to come—

YES!

Dag Hammerskjold

A Consecration to the Hearts of Jesus and Mary

Lord Jesus, Chief Shepherd of the Flock, I consecrate my life to Your Heart, pierced on Calvary for love of me. From Your pierced heart the Church was born in which I am called to give witness to your love. Help me always to pour out my life in love of God and all I meet. **Sacred Heart of Jesus, I place my trust in You.**

Dear Blessed Virgin Mary, I consecrate myself to your maternal and Immaculate Heart. You are the mother of Jesus and my mother. You are Jesus' first and perfect disciple. Teach me to imitate you in putting on Christ. Through the prayers of your Immaculate Heart, may I be guided to an ever closer union with the Heart of Christ. **Immaculate Heart of Mary, pray for me.**

A Letter from Jesus

Dear Friend,

I love you. I shed my blood for you to make you clean. You are a new creation. You are lovely in my eyes and I created you to be just as you are. Don't criticize yourself for not being perfect in your own eyes or the eyes of others. This will lead you to frustration. I want you to trust me and take one day at a time.

Dwell in my power; love, grow in freedom…be yourself. Don't allow others to run your life. I will guide you if you let me. Be aware of my presence in everything. I will give you patience, love, joy, and peace. Look to me for answers.

Come sit in my presence at the tabernacle in church. I am your shepherd and will lead you. Follow me only! Follow me in the church. Don't ever forget this.

Take some time each day to be silent. Listen to your heart and I will tell you my will. I love you. You are to love yourself and love others simply because I love you. Let my love touch everyone you meet. Take your eyes off yourself! Don't be concerned with yourself because you are my responsibility. You feel you need to change and be different. Do not worry. I will change you without your noticing it. Let me do that for you.

You are my creation. Let me have the joy of transforming your life in love. Let me give you joy, peace, and hope. No other thing or person can do this for you. Remember, you are not your own. You have been bought with my blood and are my precious possession. Surrender to my love. Don't struggle against my love. My will is perfect and will bring you peace. My love is sufficient for you. And I do love you.

Jesus

Prayer in Time of Loneliness

*Lord Jesus, you know the great pain of loneliness
because you experienced it in the Garden. At that time
you turned to your Father in prayer.
I too feel lonely and I turn to you in prayer and
I ask for your help to be with me in my pain.
It seems that I can find no friend to be with me*

or a helping hand to support me. You alone are my
support and helping hand at this time. Do
not abandon me but place me close to your most
Sacred Heart. May you give me the help and
consolation I seek. Amen.

How God Rewards Us

We can never have too much faith
and confidence in God.
God is so mighty and so merciful.
As we hope in Him so shall
we receive.
It is with love that God rewards us.

St. Thérèse Lisieux

Prayer Is...

For me, prayer is an aspiration of the heart.
Prayer is a simple glance directed to heaven.
Prayer is a cry of gratitude and love
in the midst of trial as well as joy.
Finally, it is something great and supernatural,
which expands my soul and unites me to Jesus.

St. Thérèse Lisieux

Slow Me Down, Lord!

*Slow me down, Lord. Ease the pounding of my heart by the
quieting of my mind.*

*Steady my hurried pace with a vision of the eternal reach of
time.*

*Give me, amidst the confusion of my day, the calmness of the
everlasting hills.*

*Break the tension of my nerves and muscles with the
soothing music of singing streams that live in my
memories.*

*Help me to know the magical, restorative power of your
touch.*

*Teach me the art of taking minute vacations, slowing down
to look at a flower, to chat with a friend, to pet a dog.
Remind me each day of the fable of the hare and the
tortoise so that I may know that the race is not always
won by the swift.*

There is more to life than increasing its speed.

*Let me look upward into the branches of the towering oak,
and know that it grew slowly and well.*

*Slow me down, Lord. Inspire me to send my
roots deep into the soil of life's enduring values.*

Richard Cardinal Cushing

The Rosary

The rosary is one of the most popular ways to pray and reflect on the mysteries of the Lord's life. Indeed, it is now, and has been, one of the most widely practiced devotions in the history of the Catholic Church. In praying the rosary, it is helpful to remember that it is less something to "get through" than it is a "place to go." Be at each place in these mysteries of the Lord's life. Use your imagination and invoke the Holy Spirit to help you. It is customary to pray:

The Joyful Mysteries on Monday and on Thursday (and also on Sunday—from the first Sunday of Advent until the first Sunday of Lent exclusively).

The Sorrowful Mysteries on Tuesday and Friday (and also on Sunday during Lent).

The Glorious Mysteries on Wednesday and Saturday (and also on Sunday from Easter until the first Sunday of Advent).

The Luminous Mysteries that Pope John Paul II presented to the Church in 2003 can be prayed on Thursdays. If you would like to include these new mysteries, then pray the Sorrowful, Joyful, and Glorious Mysteries on Friday, Saturday, and Sunday.

As an aid to recitation, spiritual writers have suggested certain virtues as the fruit of each mystery:

Joyful Mysteries—Spirit of Holy Joy

1. The Annunciation—Humility
2. The Visitation—Fraternal Charity

3. The Nativity—Spirit of Poverty

4. The Presentation—Obedience

5. Finding in the Temple—Love of Jesus and His Service

Sorrowful Mysteries—Spirit of Compassion and Sorrow for Sin

1. The Agony in the Garden—Fervor in Prayer

2. The Scourging at the Pillar—Penance

3. The Crowning with Thorns—Moral Courage

4. The Way of the Cross—Patience

5. The Crucifixion—A Spirit of Self-Sacrifice for God and Neighbor

The Glorious Mysteries—Spirit of Adoration and Faith

1. The Resurrection—Faith

2. The Ascension—Hope

3. Pentecost—Love and Zeal for the Salvation of Souls

4. The Assumption of the Blessed Mother—Devotion to Mary

5. The Coronation of Mary as Queen of Heaven and Earth—Final Perseverance

The Luminous Mysteries—Spirit of Discipleship

1. The Baptism of Jesus in the Jordan—Openness to Mission

2. The First Miracle of Jesus—Sanctity in Christian Marriage

3. The Proclamation of the Kingdom of God—On-Going Renewal in the Church

4. The Transfiguration—For Holy Priests and Religious

5. The Institution of the Eucharist—The Evangelization of the World

How to Pray the Rosary

1. With the crucifix, make the Sign of the Cross and pray the Apostles' Creed (see prayer below).

2. With the first bead beyond the crucifix, pray the Our Father.

3. With the next three beads, pray the Hail Mary on each; one for faith, one for hope, one for charity. After the three Hail Marys, pray the Glory Be. (Repeat 4 through 6 for each of the five mysteries: Joyful, Sorrowful, and Glorious. A mystery includes one bead for the Our Father, and ten beads for ten Hail Marys.)

4. On the last of the beads before the three-way joint, announce the first mystery and pray the Our Father.

5. Beginning with the first bead on the left beyond the three-way joint, pray ten Hail Marys, one for each bead. After the last Hail Mary, pray the Glory Be.

6. After the Glory Be, many Catholics pray the prayer taught to the children of Fatima by the angel:

"Oh my Jesus, forgive us our sins, save us from the fires of hell and bring all souls to heaven, especially those most in need of your mercy."

7. Proceed to the next mystery and repeat the process, but focus your heart on the new grace of our Lord's life that the mystery entails while you pray the prayers.

8. After the conclusion of the fifth mystery, pray the Hail Holy Queen.

9. Concluding Prayer:

O God whose only begotten Son, by his life, death, and resurrection has purchased for us the rewards of eternal salvation, grant, we beseech thee, that by meditating upon the mysteries of the most Holy Rosary of the Blessed Virgin Mary, we may imitate what they contain and obtain what they promise, through the same Christ, Our Lord. Amen.

Close with the Sign of the Cross, using the crucifix of the rosary. Many offer one Our Father, Hail Mary, and a Glory Be at the conclusion of each rosary for the needs and intentions of the Holy Father.

Prayers of the Rosary

The Apostles' Creed

I believe in God, the Father almighty, creator of heaven and earth. I believe in Jesus Christ, his only Son, our Lord. He was conceived by the power of the Holy Spirit and born of the Virgin Mary. He suffered under Pontius Pilate, was crucified, died and was buried. He descended to the dead, and on the third day, rose again. He ascended into heaven, and is seated at the right hand of the Father. He will come again to judge the living and the dead. I believe in the Holy Spirit, the Holy Catholic Church, the communion of saints, the forgiveness of sins, the resurrection of the body, and life everlasting. Amen.

Our Father

Our Father, who art in heaven, hallowed by the name: Thy Kingdom come, thy will be done, on earth as it is in heaven. Give us this day, our daily bread, and forgive us our trespasses, as we forgive those who trespass against us; and lead us not into temptation, but deliver us from evil. Amen.

Hail Mary

Hail Mary, full of grace, the Lord is with thee. Blessed art thou among women, and blessed is the fruit of thy womb, Jesus. Holy Mary, Mother of God, pray for us sinners, now and at the hour of our death. Amen.

Glory Be

Glory be to the Father, and to the Son, and to the Holy Spirit. As it was in the beginning, is now and ever shall be, world without end. Amen.

Hail Holy Queen

Hail Holy Queen, Mother of Mercy, our life, our sweetness, and our hope. To thee do we cry, poor banished children of Eve. To thee do we send up our cries, mourning and weeping in this valley of tears. Turn then, O most Gracious Advocate, thine eyes of mercy toward us, and after this our exile, show unto us the Blessed Fruit of Thy womb, Jesus. O clement, O loving, O sweet Virgin Mary. Pray for us O Holy Mother of God, that we may be made worthy of the promises of Christ. Amen.

My Mission of Service

God has created me to do him some definite service; he has committed some work to me which he has not committed to another. I have my mission—I may never know it in this life, but I shall be told it in the next.

I am a link in a chain, a bond of connection between persons. God has not created me for naught. I shall do good. I shall do his work. I shall be an angel of peace, a preacher of truth in my own place while not intending it—if I do but keep God's Commandments.

Therefore, I will trust God, whatever, wherever I am. I can never be thrown away. If I am in sickness, my sickness may serve God; in perplexity my perplexity may serve God, if I am in sorrow, my sorrow may serve God. God knows what he is about. God may take my friends or throw me among strangers. God may make me feel desolate, make my spirits sink, hide my future from me—still God knows what he is about. God does nothing in vain.

A Meditation by Cardinal Newman

The Glorified Christ

Glorious Lord Christ: the divine influence secretly diffused and active in the depths of matter, and the dazzling center where all the innumerable fibers of the manifold meet; power as implacable as the world and as warm as life; you whose forehead is of the whiteness of snow, whose eyes are of fire, and whose feet are brighter than molten gold; you whose hands imprison the stars; you are the first and the last, the living and the dead and the risen again; you who gather into your exuberant unity every beauty, every affinity, every energy, every mode of existence; it is you to whom my being cried out with a desire as vast as the universe, "In truth your are my Lord and my God."

Teilhard de Chardin